Leaving the MOTHER SHIP

Having the courage to leave,
and charting the path to get there

Randall M. Craig

Leaving the MOTHER SHIP

Having the courage to leave,
and charting the path to get there

Knowledge to Action Press
Toronto - New York - London

Leaving the Mother Ship

Published by Knowledge to Action Press

Knowledge to Action Press
602 Glengrove Avenue
Toronto ON Canada M6B 2H8
www.KnowledgeToActionPress.com

Printed in Canada

Book layout and cover design by Swerve Design Group Inc.
Author photograph by Laura Arsie Photography

Library and Archives Canada Cataloguing in Publication

Craig, Randall M., 1963-
Leaving the mother ship : having the courage to leave, and charting the path to get there / Randall M. Craig.

ISBN 0-9735404-0-0

1. Career changes. 2. Career development. I. Title.

HF5384.C72 2004 650.14 C2004-902928-2

SPECIAL SALES
This book is available with special discounts for bulk purchases if used for educational, promotional, or business uses. For information, please email specialsales@KnowledgeToActionPress.com, and provide the book title and ISBN, how it will be used, quantity, and date required.

For Linda, Shale, Jacqueline, and Sabrina

The only thing that separates you from achievement is time, and how you use it.

Contents

Acknowledgments

- To my very talented wife Linda, who is simultaneously my toughest critic and strongest supporter. Her insightful comments have added immeasurably to this book.
- To my three children, Shale, Jacqueline, and Sabrina: for their fresh perspective and the wide-ranging discussions we've had about the working world.
- To John Craig, a tremendous example of fatherhood, doing the right thing, and business acumen. And to my mother, Evvie Craig, who always shared her kitchen wisdom generously.
- To Bob "Coach" Coffey, who helped me with my "first MBA" and taught me, by example, what a professional work week really meant. He also deserves credit for introducing me to the Bluebird, and how to Fish where the fish are.
- To Denis Ho and M-C Shanahan: both excellent managers whose unique styles and aptitudes were exemplary. And who both successfully left the Mother Ship.
- To the very few inept managers I've known, who tirelessly shared, by example, how not to manage.
- To my many former colleagues, too many to mention here, who challenged me as a manager, and always became trusted friends.
- To those who have led interesting careers and have shared them with me over the years: Mike Davis, Alan Feldman, Annette Frymer, Larry Goldberg, Yechiel Goldreich, John Hempsey, Mishka Ilmer, Jacki Jenuth, Jordan Kalpin, Andrew Kirby, Ethan Kohn, Joe and Kim Morrison, Amir Raubvogel, Sandy Salem, Sandra Shaul, Les Slotin, Bruce Winstanley and Cheryl Zeldin. And to the dozens of others who also left a bit of themselves on the pages that follow, by sharing their stories and advice.

- To my many clients over the years who asked for my help with their business challenges. And to those same ones who asked for my advice with their career planning.
- To Dr. Elliott Malamet, who thought I was helping him with Project E. He was really helping me with Project R, even though I didn't know it at the time.
- To Dr. Burt Konzak, a master storyteller, author, and my karate sensei.
- To Greg Secker: attitude, and not just aptitude, achieves altitude.
- To those who helped me learn to write; especially Michael Pieri, a one-of-a-kind newspaperman, and Gordon Braun-Woodbury, an exceptionally talented communications professional.
- To Mark Haak and David Johnson of Swerve Design Group, and my editor, Wendy Thomas.
- To Paul Koven, who proved that at the age of 62, you're never too old to start, then finish, a graduate degree. And who was taken by cancer the year after he graduated.
- To all the people who reviewed the draft and provided so many useful comments. If I have missed mentioning you by name, my sincerest apologies. I hope that a nice dinner can make it up to you.

Foreword

I have much respect for the author of this book. Not only has he been a tremendous coach and inspiration to work with over the years, he has been involved with some of the most meteoric successes in my career. What Randall Craig doesn't know or hasn't discovered in the realms of business planning, marketing, or career mastery probably isn't worth knowing. Since our early heady days of building one of the first multibillion-dollar web-based money market businesses from simple means in Toronto, Canada, we have kept in touch over the years, comparing trends in the U.K. and North America.

It was when Randall was in London in 2001 that I really discovered he was onto something. We met for dinner at an Indian restaurant just south of the eclectic area of Soho. As we discussed the business issues of the day, he gave me a gift. I had asked him, "So… when is the right time to leave your job?" The response was swift and exacting, and delivered with such passion and intensity, the napkin on which he scribbled barely remained intact. When someone delivers this type of message, you know it isn't something they have read, but something they have lived. This formula, the *Job Quality Checklist*, is one of several now in the book. It is as follows:

1. Are you having fun?
2. Are you being challenged intellectually?
3. Do you like your colleagues?
4. Are you reaching your career goals?
5. Are you achieving life balance?
6. Is your compensation somewhat close to your worth?

The resonance and congruency of his message made me recognize that it was time to make a change. As our discussions progressed, and as you'll discover in the book, the implications of this knowledge are often more profound than they initially appear. By answering the questions (and doing the other exercises) I was able to channel my energies productively and develop a much tighter focus.

For myself, after many years of successfully running on-line trading rooms for large institutional banks and financial services firms, I wanted out. Given my background in training, and from the years modeling and managing some of the best traders around the world, I felt compelled to make these same skills accessible to private individuals. I found my passion in providing pragmatic investment training for those serious about creating wealth, and left the Mother Ship. My path crossed Randall's once again: the Secker Investment Institute was born, and I haven't looked back since.

We live in a time when we recognize that we must control our own destiny – financial, career, and otherwise. As successful managers thinking about leaving for the first time, we are no longer willing to delegate control over our lives to employers, financial institutions, or the government.

Leaving the Mother Ship is a road map – a set of empowerment tools – that you can immediately use to set your own direction. It can help you acknowledge that perhaps the future "on the inside" is no longer the only alternative. It can help you recognize that to achieve your destiny, now is the time to be honest, to be prepared, and to act.

If you have any question about deciding, planning, timing, or surviving before and after you leave your Mother Ship, this is the book for you. It is a pragmatic masterpiece and essential reading. As you carry out the exercises and understand the strategies, you'll discover the sense of empowerment that only comes when you have a clear goal in mind.

Greg Secker
London, England

Introduction

Let's face it. We spend more time at our "day jobs" than anywhere else. For this reason, it is important that we find our days satisfying, both mentally and financially. Yet how often is this not the case? Sometimes we find ourselves locked into a job on a career path that is not of our own choosing. Sometimes politics and stupidity (both ours and others') distract us, long after we've driven home. Sometimes we are so driven by our jobs that there is no home life at all.

Yet as successful managers, we are driven to succeed. We are promoted before our peers into areas of greater responsibility; we work with exciting and smart people, and love the rush of our success. We travel for both business and pleasure, enjoy more exclusive perks, and enjoy the fruits of our labor – when there is time. At a certain point, however, we begin to question whether the next job in our career should remain within the organization that "made us" or whether, for the first time, we should consider leaving the Mother Ship.

How can we figure this out, especially since each person's circumstances are unique? By starting where there is commonality, and then using a process that can help better frame your personal plan:

1. **KNOWING WHEN TO GO:** Benchmark your starting point, then review key criteria to answer this question.
2. **KNOWING WHERE TO GO:** What are the options? Look at the pros and cons of each, and where you might be best suited to look. Buff up your weaknesses, and leverage your strengths.
3. **SUCCESS BEYOND THE MOTHER SHIP:** Now that you've left the Mother Ship, what are the most common mistakes, and how do you avoid them? And how do you plan for what comes next?

Maybe you're ready to go now, or maybe you've decided just to explore the idea for a while. This book will give you the information, perspective, and courage to make the right decision.

A final warning – and a piece of advice: Leaving the Mother Ship isn't easy, and your success beyond it certainly isn't guaranteed. The probability of being successful very much depends upon your strength of mind: master that, and you can master anything.

Throughout this book, you will find a number of diagnostic exercises that help you understand when and where to go. If you skip them, you will have a less than honest appraisal of when or where to go. More importantly, you will miss an opportunity to develop your strength of mind – precisely what you need after you leave. Spend the time doing the exercises – the discipline you earn will pay off handsomely.

PART I:

Knowing When to Go

Knowing when to go: the big question. Your answer may be "Not soon enough!" or it may be "Eventually." The only difference between these answers is time. And the only difference between those who think about going and those who actually go is courage. Taking control over your career – even just buying this book – is empowering. But can you be successful off the Mother Ship? Do you have the right skills to succeed? And how do you know when to go?

These are the questions that this part of the book will start answering. We'll consider your current environment, your current skill base, and introduce a tool (the Job Quality Checklist) that defines criteria to evaluate your current position – and your next one. Finally, we'll look at triggering events – indicators that can tell you when it's time to go.

Chapter 1: Problems with the Status Quo

We spend more time at work, or thinking about work, than pretty much any other activity in life. Why is it then, that many people are not excited about getting up out of bed each morning and going to work? Clearly, this is an indicator that something is wrong. We realize this instinctively, yet we don't do anything about it. What is pushing us to make a change just now? Are we running *to* our next challenge, or are we running *from* something else instead? Defining the problem is usually the first step in solving it.

What Is the Problem?

You may believe that the "problem" is related to determining the next step in your career: after all, you did buy this book. But it is important to recognize, and possibly rule out, other factors that may be obscuring the picture. For some people, these factors are distractions, which should rightfully be ignored, whereas for others, these factors are exactly what must be addressed. Unless they are addressed (or ruled out), the very same job dissatisfaction will continue to come up, time and time again.

Let's look at some of the typical problem areas.

Life Velocity

When speaking to retirees about my typical day, they are amazed at how much is going on. They are glad to be away from the rat race; they don't know how we do it.[1] The velocity of our lives is incredible.

Let's look at the modern rat race a bit more closely. After some degree of success you likely have a house or condo of your own, a car or two, a membership at a health club (and possibly also a golf club); your children may go to a private school, but whether they do or not, they are certainly involved in dance,

1. Interestingly, this is similar to the married person saying to their single friends, "I'm glad I'm no longer single – the bar scene, dating, I don't know how you do it!"

piano, karate, swimming, and tennis. Thankfully, your spouse can help with the children, but your spouse needs some of your time too. Your commute to work takes at least an hour of your day – if you're not on a road trip meeting clients or suppliers. Your mortgage and other financial commitments are almost overwhelming; your time obligations surely are. And all of this on top of your job responsibilities.

You think to yourself, "How did I get myself into this situation?" Like the retirees, you say to yourself, "I'm so busy, I don't know how I do it!" But do it you must, because if you stop, you worry about not being able to start up again. There just isn't enough time in the day!

Time is needed for both reflection and planning.

Despite all these competing pressures, there are many ways to mitigate the problem of velocity. If you are considering leaving the Mother Ship, time is needed for both reflection and planning. And there are a number of important, but time-consuming activities that need to be done. Time is also needed to read this book! To manufacture some time, you either need to change your current priorities, become more productive, or cut things from your schedule. Here are a few suggestions that might help:

- **BUILD EXERCISE INTO YOUR ROUTINE.** Not only will this reduce your general stress level, but you will look better and feel better, and your body will last longer. Even though exercise takes time away from your day, you will return to work more alert and more productive.
- **TAKE A 24-HOUR VACATION EACH WEEK.** Remember the concept of *a day of rest?* Why not institutionalize it in your life? Recharge your batteries by not working, not shopping, not answering your cell phone, and not using your computer one day each week.
- **SCHEDULE "FOCUS TIME."** Give yourself permission to take some time each day specifically for thinking and reflection. Personally, I do my best thinking when I'm exercising. Not consciously thinking, but letting my brain work on a problem in the background. For you, it may be some other

way, but it is certain that your best "thinking" time is not when you have phones ringing, emails chiming, or deadlines imminently looming. Unless we cordon off time each day specifically for thinking and reflection, it is unlikely that we will actually think or reflect.

- **GO TO A DAY SPA.** It's surprising what some concentrated pampering can do to your state of mind.
- **TAKE YOUR VACATIONS!** Think about your vacation entitlements: do you take all the vacation that you earn? If you don't take at least three weeks off each year, over time, you'll probably burn yourself out. Personally, I always planned my vacations in places where I couldn't be reached: hiking in the Canadian Rockies, for example. Travel, even locally, can give you a whole new perspective.
- **TAKE AN EXTENDED VACATION OR SABBATICAL.** University professors have known about the rejuvenating impact of a short-term change of pace for many years. Why can't you do the same? Consider how taking a month (or three) off can improve your perspective.

Later in this book, we'll look more deeply at the issue of achieving balance, and the connection to career choice. For now, the objective is simply to capture enough time to reflect and plan.

Spouse and Family Problems

How often do you come home from a tough day at work and "take it out" on the spouse and kids? Or clam up, and don't do or say anything until it's too late? When you have a great day, it shows, and everyone is happy with the family's collective good fortune. If you have an awful day and blow up, everyone (including yourself) feels bad. We oscillate between these two poles, although not always to the extremes.

Consider: What if our home life is not positive or supportive? What is the impact when we go into work after a big fight, or with news that our children are failing in school, or with news that a parent has just been diagnosed with a terrible disease? There is *always* an impact.

We might take it out on our co-workers and become known as a hardass. Or maybe a relationship with a supporting co-worker blooms inappropriately. Or maybe we smother ourselves in our work and pretend that no problems exist at home (and thereby exacerbate the very problem that our attention requires). When times are bad, we need to look to our spouse and children for support, but we sometimes find it difficult to do so because we are so out of practice.

Don't divorce the family because of the job, nor quit the job because of a problem in the family.

No matter how much we might try, dissatisfaction (or satisfaction) at home will affect the job, and vice versa. No matter how you look at it – glass half-full or glass half-empty – you shouldn't divorce the family because of the job, nor quit the job because of a problem in the family. Solve the problem at its root, or it will surely repeat itself on the next go-round.

Job Velocity

A friend, top of his class in engineering and one of the brightest lights in his Ivy League law class, decided to interview at major New York law firms for one of the coveted first-year technology law positions. As was done in this type of situation, my friend was interviewed by about a dozen partners and associates during the day, one after the other. The office was beautiful, it had a busy excitement that was equally alluring, and the pay, especially at the beginning, was lucrative.

He was shown into the first interviewer's office; the interviewer described working life and painted a picture of a firm that "works hard and plays hard." The next person he met was also very positive on the organization, as was the third, who noted that the firm brought in a catered dinner when a team was working late on a deal.

My friend noticed, however, that behind each office door there was a thin futon standing upright; he decided to ask what it was for. The answer? If you have to work through the night, the futon can be used to sleep on, so as to minimize transit time. The next person told him that a fresh shirt is purchased for each person after an all-nighter. The next told him about the great breakfasts that are catered after all-nighters. And so on.

The postscript: He could have had the prestige and financial rewards of a top New York firm, but at what cost? After hearing from his boastful would-be colleagues how great the firm was, he decided that this wasn't the place for him. Instead, he has had an excellent career at a top-notch firm in California, living, working, and raising a family there for the last 15 years.

While this story is amusing, consider what has happened to the velocity of business over this time period. At one time, faxes were sent only for urgent materials; there was no email, nor voicemail; senior executives often used "secretaries" for both dictation and personal errands. Today, it is not uncommon for some managers to receive 50 to 75 (and more) emails per day, as well as dozens of voicemails. And when we are out of the office, we have these systems programmed to auto-reply or forward to our cell phones. Some people put only their cell phone number on their business cards and then don't turn the cell phones off at the end of the day. In some organizations, the use of instant messaging, screen sharing, and two-way text pagers are creating whole new ways to be accessible – and interrupted.

There are some advantages to this huge increase in velocity: improved customer service, better risk management, and better resource utilization. In fact, if it weren't for cell phone calls to our spouses while in transit, many a marriage would have been ruined! The pressure of speed is not a problem in and of itself – but the problem is who or what is in control. If you don't control the velocity, it will control you. Here are some simple suggestions, once again given to help you find time for planning and reflection:

If you don't control the velocity, it will control you.

- Set firm time boundaries. For example, resolve not to work after 10 p.m. or before 7 a.m.
- Consider, for example, your increased productivity (and reduced stress) if you limited email access to two to three times per day, rather than "instant response."

- Just as you likely do with paper that crosses your desk, prioritize tasks that come in through these new channels (e.g., voicemail, email, mobile text messaging, instant messaging) and deal with them according to your priorities and timing.
- Consider forwarding your cell phone to voicemail both during meetings and when you require uninterrupted time to think. Turn your cell phone off at night.
- Consider again the impact if you took 15 minutes each morning, before you got onto the job treadmill, just for yourself. This *focus time* could be used to help set your daily priorities both in the context of your day job and your Leaving the Mother Ship activities.

Are you catching up on your work only at night and over each weekend?

Notwithstanding these suggestions, it's important to understand how job velocity has suddenly crept up on you. Do you (or others) believe that you are irreplaceable in your job? Are you catching up on your work only at night and over each weekend?

As an executive at an international public company, I would talk to our clients about the benefits of being a global organization, and our ability to work on problems 24 hours each day. For example, if an issue came up in North America, it could be solved by the lab overseas while North America slept. I and others would describe the benefits of throwing the work "over the fence" at the end of our business day and arrive the next morning to see the problem solved, in our email boxes.

The reality, though, was a bit different. At about midnight, the email traffic from the early risers in the U.K. would start. By 2 a.m., the rest of Europe and the Middle East would add their traffic. To ensure that the problem got solved, you would respond to the emails as they came in. Meanwhile, others would see that you were on-line, as you all use the same instant messenger program. You open a chat window to discuss the issues in real time. But typing is inconvenient, and the language gap makes communications this way cumbersome; before long, you're on the phone. Emails are still streaming in, though, and others are opening chat windows to you, asking "quick" questions. And you're still on the phone. All this at 2 a.m.

In this situation, the increased velocity was caused by the promise to the client. But the velocity was made far worse because no firm time boundaries were set.

If you really think you are managing yourself efficiently, and most people do, perhaps the problem is more about poorly managed behavioral norms in the organization. Typical examples include emails that are time-stamped throughout the night, and persistent cell phone calls after 10 p.m. If this is the case and you don't want to (or can't) swim upstream to effect change, one of the solutions is to leave the Mother Ship. Either the organization must change or you should.

Culture of the Organization

The organization that you joined those many years ago had a distinct culture. For some reason, it is now different: a customer-centric view of the world may have changed to one that is focused only on quarterly results. A reputation for technology leadership may have changed to one that doesn't value research and development. A hard-driving competitive environment has changed into one that seems slow and complacent. Or perhaps the standards of integrity have slipped down a notch. Whatever the reason, the changes don't sit well with you.

Maybe the culture hasn't changed, but it is you who has matured over the years.

If you are in a position of leadership, consider how this change has occurred: quickly, because of a particular event, or slowly, because of an evolutionary slide? If the latter, as a senior manager, you must take some responsibility for it.

Maybe the culture hasn't changed, but it is you who has matured over the years. No longer young and naive, you have developed a growing discomfort with the culture, and you realize that this discomfort will only worsen with time.

While you are still with the organization, is it a worthwhile management challenge to move the culture to something that is positive (and therefore acceptable to you)? Perhaps. But once again, in the end, either the organization must change, or you should. Otherwise, it is time to leave the Mother Ship.

KEY POINTS

- Life is full of challenges: some are at home, and some are at work. Recognize these challenges for what they are, then consider how you can address them.
- Don't quit your job because of a problem in the family; likewise, don't lose your family because of a problem at the job.
- To successfully leave the Mother Ship, you need time to think and reflect. Give yourself permission to take some time, each day, to do this.

Chapter 2: Large Organizations: The "Home" We Know Best

What makes a larger organization work well for some of us? And what are the downsides? Since these are the animals we know best, and since our success has been predicated partly on our organizational knowledge, it is worthwhile examining their pros and cons.

Reasons We Love the Large Organization

1. Organizational Process and People Knowledge

As you move up the organizational ladder, your internal network and knowledge grow hugely. Your credibility with your colleagues and subordinates lets you get things done more easily than others, and you always know who to call when your staff presents you with a problem that needs solving.

While this is certainly positive for you as an individual, organizations are now seeing the other side: with lowered employee loyalty, your knowledge is also an area of risk. What if the only person who understands a certain process leaves? Or if Jennifer, the only one who understands the history of client X, gets hired by a competitor?

Years ago, I was helping a large media company with its Internet strategy. A critical piece of the strategy was the integration of its mainframe with its yet-to-be-developed web site. As it turned out, we discovered an area of terribly high risk for the company. One programmer – an older man – was the only one left in the whole company who understood the arcane programming and logic of the mainframe. What would happen if the programmer retired (or died) before the knowledge was transferred? Whoops.

One of the more interesting trends today is that of *Knowledge Management* (KM). We certainly like the idea of being called *knowledge workers*, and as leaders, the idea of managing a *learning organization* is flattering. KM seeks to extract organizational knowledge, automate it, and make it available to anyone within the organization, when they need it. The promise of each of us working up to our potential, with the lubricating comfort of others' knowledge, is satisfying.

Make sure that you work to maximize your external value.

This does not bode well for those who put all their eggs exclusively into the basket of internal knowledge. Organizations breed workers who are often better at working the system than they are at their jobs. Consider yourself: If you know exactly how to fudge "the system" to get things done, what is your value outside your organization? Unfortunately, very little. If you are known as a very strong internal networker, and your value is "hooking up" the right people within your organization, what is your value outside your organization? Also, very little. On the other hand, if you honestly have developed strong people skills (e.g., leadership, mentoring, evaluation), your people knowledge is a benefit from an underlying skill, and not the other way around. The result is a higher external value.

A former grad school colleague found herself in this type of a situation, but was able to spin it completely to her advantage. She worked at one of the largest financial institutions in the country and through a series of promotions held a senior position. She was looking to make a change, but was concerned that too much of her value was tied up in her internal "system" knowledge and personal relationships.

She realized that she would have to limit her job search to companies that valued her system knowledge and internal relationships as highly as her business acumen. In the end, she found a senior level position working at a supplier to her former employer: her old department became her client. She turned a definite weakness into something that clearly differentiated her from other candidates.

The upshot is simple: if you are considering leaving the Mother Ship, make sure that you work to maximize your external value. If you are a bit light in this area, it's time to bulk up; otherwise, be prepared for both higher risk and narrower choices when you leave.

2. Tremendous Support Systems

Once beyond their egos, most successful managers and entrepreneurs will attribute their success to the team they work with: their subordinates, peers, and managers. We rely on these people to make decisions on our behalf, exercise judgment, and point out when our decisions don't make sense. Their success often means our success. And when we work with them for many years, the collective team begins to develop a strong understanding of each other, personally and professionally.

Often, the value of a mentor is their organizational knowledge coupled with their interest in you.

Separately from the people, support departments await our beck and call. Computer doesn't work? Call IT. Questions about a payroll change? Call HR. Reports to copy, bind, and then deliver? Call the mailroom. Need some giveaways for a new client meeting? Call Marketing. Each of these areas (and others like them) are staffed with specialized and trained people. Each area has preferential deals with a host of suppliers.

We also receive support from our mentors. How often have they steered us through difficult decisions? Or put in a good word for us when it really counted? Often, the value of a mentor is their organizational knowledge coupled with their interest in you. If you were to leave the organization, the nature of the relationship may change. If you have a mentor outside, then you are fortunate indeed: leaving the Mother Ship can leave the mentor relationship intact.

The large organization is a fully functioning entity, organized in a self-supporting web of relationships, support departments, and systems. It has helped you become efficient in your day job and has allowed you to develop the focus necessary for a successful career. If you move to another Mother Ship, be prepared to relearn where these support systems can be found. If you follow an entrepreneurial path, be prepared to personally learn how these support systems work as you undertake each time-consuming task yourself.

3. Multiple Career Path Options

"Up or out" is the mantra at most consulting firms. And at smaller companies, promotion is very difficult because of long staff retention and the problem of successful succession. For different reasons, career options are a bit stifled in both types of organizations. But in most larger organizations there are many appealing paths that can stem from any one position.

Assume that you've gone through a period in sales and are now at the Director of Sales level. Your next move might be to the Vice-president of Sales. But it could also be to a number of other worthwhile positions:

- Director of Sales for a more strategic portfolio of accounts.
- Director of Marketing.
- Director in charge of special projects.
- A mid-senior role in another geographic region.

Each of these positions, although possibly lateral moves, would give you special skills that would ultimately position you for an even more senior role, either internally or externally. Large organizations give you several internal options for promotion; smaller companies might provide only one.

4. Job Security

We like to think that working in a larger organization gives us a degree of job security. The reality, however, is another matter.

We like to think that working in a larger organization gives us a degree of job security that smaller organizations just are not able to provide. Insolvency is usually not a daily worry, nor is meeting payroll. As a more senior manager, we are often the ones making the decisions, not just being affected by them.

The reality, however, is another matter. While some may have predicted the Internet technology crash several years ago, very few could have predicted the impact of an extended recession or the accounting scandals. Furthermore, unless you consistently exceed your objectives, someone somewhere within the organization is likely saying that you should be replaced with someone who can make it happen faster. "More" job security than others? Maybe not!

On the other hand, when we are let go we often receive lucrative severance packages. And depending on the jurisdiction, there may even be government-mandated minimums. To be laid off and still get paid for two, three, or twelve months is comforting. And this severance is possible, really, only at larger organizations.

5. A Title That Looks Good on the Résumé: What's in a Name Matters

When you are interviewing candidates for a position, are you more or less likely to give consideration to someone who comes from a recognized brand name? You think to yourself, if they could make it at IBM, then they could make it at your company. Otherwise, you think to yourself, they would have been fired long ago.

The brand equity of a recognized company rubs off on its employees, effectively guaranteeing that they meet a minimum standard of quality. Your employer's name gives you some bragging rights – you've made the cut, and others haven't.

Your employer's name gives you some bragging rights – you've made the cut, and others haven't.

Titles do a similar thing. Does a person have what it takes to be the president? If they were a president before, they can do it again. And to be honest, there usually is some degree of satisfaction when looking at your own business card with the title Director, VP, or President.

Summary

Process and people knowledge. Support systems. Big Company career path. Security. Big Company name and title. Are you prepared to make a change and possibly give them up? What would your days look like without IT support, or without your assistant? How would you feel working for a company that didn't have a "name"? Or without the people that you've spent 10 or more years working with? To a certain degree, each has contributed to your success. How would you feel about starting all over again, having to earn credibility with your new colleagues from day one? Recognizing what change might mean is the first step in reducing your surprise after you have left.

Reasons We Hate the Large Organization

We chuckle at the foibles of characters on television or in comic strips, but groan at how close some of the situations are to our own. Large organizations, by their nature, are imperfect. If you are considering leaving, is it because of these imperfections, or because your drive is taking you somewhere else? If it is because of an organizational problem, recognize it as such. Doing so will help you avoid the same problem elsewhere.

There are many reasons why we might not "appreciate" the larger organization; here are a few:

1. Bureaucracy and Process

Process is a very good thing: it instills fairness and order, and helps institutionalize accountability. The problems start, however, when there is so little empowerment in the bureaucracy that the rules become an end in themselves. Rather than common sense, policies and procedures often get in the way of meeting customers' and other stakeholders' needs.

I recall consulting to a major financial institution several years ago. A manager was describing to me the internal policies and procedures that governed their working days. The policies were printed out and put in binders for easy reference. These binders filled two shelving units, eight feet wide.[2] While some of the regulations were probably government mandated, and others were internal audit requirements, I just couldn't believe the sheer volume of them. No wonder so many large institutions have poor reputations for customer service. Who could possibly remember all the policies and procedures, let alone the reasons for them!

Another example: Much earlier in my career, I was "put up" for promotion by the national partner-in-charge of my area. I had excelled in every assigned responsibility and was doing the job of the senior position to boot. Unfortunately, my appointment was vetoed by the HR department. The reason?

---

2. Today, of course, intranets have greatly reduced the need for policy binders and storage shelves, but the policies and procedures still exist, hidden within intranet sites.

The firm's policy was that people had to remain in their position for at least three years before being considered for promotion. I had been a manager for "only" two; therefore I was not "eligible" – end of story. The fact that I had earned the promotion in the eyes of my manager was irrelevant.

In the end, I was able to mobilize a number of allies in senior management to successfully fight on my behalf and get the promotion pushed through. The experience left a foul taste in my mouth, but it taught me first-hand how destructive policy and procedure can be if left in the hands of non-thinkers. It also started me thinking about the importance of taking a personal interest in setting my career direction. Clearly, delegating control over my career to others wasn't in my best interest!

2. Refuge of the Mediocre

How many below-average people are in your organization? Likely, the answer is too many. The reason? With little recognition for their achievements, the best people leave. The average people are the ones who usually end up making up the rules to perpetuate this system, and the below-average ones hide in the reeds, putting in their time. While in most organizations there are *some* stars who stay (this likely includes you!), the make-up of the team is highly weighted to the mediocre. Ask any coach: it is tough to make a good team with those who put in their time, but not their spirit.

With little recognition for their achievements, the best people leave.

It is frustrating to see potential unrealized by a seeming lack of motivation, effort, or commitment. Whether you see it in others, or recognize that you are slowly losing the spark yourself, the reasons for it are unique to each individual. Nevertheless, consider the following possibility: lack of motivation at work might indicate that they have priorities focused elsewhere – perhaps in the community, or with a sick relative. Another possibility: they just don't enjoy their job but don't have the courage or knowledge to seek change.

As someone who has been successful working within the organization, why does this matter to you? Simple: over time, you will become more and more like your colleagues, which may mean, unfortunately, mediocre and below average. If you don't like what your colleagues look like now, don't look in the mirror a few years down the road, as you won't like what you see there either.

3. Political Wolves

When a request comes your way, what immediately comes to mind?

"Okay, let's do it!" or

- "Why is he asking?"
- "What's in it for me?"
- "I'll say yes, and then do nothing, just to get him off my back."
- "Can I screw him? Last time he didn't help me out."
- And only then… "What was that request again?"

Whether politics translates into obstacle-making, backstabbing, or opportunism, it does get in the way. Why do people play politics anyway, especially when it is hurtful and dysfunctional to the team?

"Take the credit, give the blame."

It is a natural thing to not only do your job, but ensure that your manager knows that you did it. Unfortunately, some corporate cultures are set up to be so competitive that some managers believe that to get ahead requires winners (them) and losers (anyone else). A political wolf's credo is simple: "Take the credit, give the blame." Others play politics because they believe that stepping on others can only make them look better. Or they have such low self-esteem that only by being hurtful to others can they feel satisfied themselves.

The problem with political wolves appears when their aggressive behavior undermines you, and weakens your position in the fold. That you have to spend an increasing amount of your time playing the game and protecting your back is partly what you find uncomfortable. If only the wolves spent as much time on their day jobs as they did on gossip, spin, and positioning.

4. Image Managers

Some people within the organization are more concerned about ego and personal positioning than the business. Perhaps they wear the flashiest clothes, or perhaps not. But they spend more time on how the PowerPoint presentation looks than on the content of the presentation itself. And they make sure to leave voicemails and emails for as many people as possible when they work on the weekend. While every organization needs its motivational speakers, nobody should be left asking the question "Where's the beef?"

5. One-Dimensional Wonders

We sometimes find the one-dimensional wonder among the most driven "A-type" personalities. They are concerned only about work. They don't have strong relationships beyond those at the office. They are so focused on the task that they forget the human element, of their customers or their colleagues. When in a position of authority, they are often ruthless in their drive and alienate the very people they should be motivating. Their negative energy certainly gets things done, but it isn't the environment that you signed up for.

The longer you work with them, the more you become like them.

There is another, sadder, side to these people. Several years ago, a workmate brought her newborn baby to the office. Quickly, a number of people congregated around, poking and prodding the baby. The two people who had the most joy were the one-dimensional people that I had written off in my mind much earlier. All of them were highly successful professionally, but were either unmarried or past child-bearing years. It was very sad indeed.

More worrisome is what will happen to those who work with one-dimensional wonders: the longer you work with them, the more you become like them.

6. The Stupid Ones

Do you find yourself having to explain your requirements to your colleagues over and over to gain understanding? Does your patience wane when others don't "get it" as fast as you? While nobody is the perfect communicator, some organizations have either over-promoted too many people or have recruiting policies that dip toward the bottom of the intellectual barrel. If you are in a family business, nepotism doesn't help, either.

Stupid ones are terribly efficient at developing roadblocks and preventing action.

Whatever the reason, you may be becoming frustrated by these people. They can become terribly efficient at developing roadblocks and preventing action.

Before jumping on the "Exactly!" bandwagon, here's a suggestion: consider that, just maybe, these people see you as patronizing and arrogant, and are only acting stupid to annoy you. Before accepting that your organization has the "stupid ones" problem, try to reason how you would both change others' perceptions of you, and ultimately fix the problem. When you leave the Mother Ship, the same issue may dodge you wherever you land; test-driving a solution immediately gives you invaluable experience.

7. The Hoarders

Several years ago, a salesperson in my organization told me, "Don't worry, Randall, the prospects will be calling in the next three weeks: my system works." Salespeople have used this line, or a version of it, forever. What is this much-vaunted system? It usually is a bunch of wheel-spinning, calls, faxes, and meetings, but unless there is transparency to the process, and until there are results, it is just smoke and mirrors. How can you deal with this obfuscation? Call them on it: tell them that the time of Secret Sauce is over, and they now have to open up and reveal their ingredients.

The salesperson, in this example, is a hoarder. Hoarders seek to differentiate themselves with knowledge that no one else has. The disease strikes people throughout the organization, from people who hoard knowledge on a customer, to those who hoard knowledge about a product, a supplier relationship, a production machine, a piece of software, or even what's happening within the organization.

What if your boss is a hoarder? Early in my career, I worked in a department run by one. The most senior executive had access to all information. In his schema, senior managers got less, and managers got even less. Analysts got pretty much nothing, and the support staff were pretty much invisible. All this information segregation, and there were only about 15 people in the group! Human nature being what it is, many people spent time guessing what was happening, filling in the blanks with worst-case scenarios, and often making their decisions with incomplete data. A boss who is a hoarder is particularly difficult – you're effectively being controlled by your lack of knowledge. A general rule: the more senior someone is, the more transparency is required. Unfortunately, the exact opposite is usually the case.

Hoarders seek to differentiate themselves with knowledge that no one else has.

Interestingly, hoarders are the flip-side to one of the major advantages of a large organization: your unique knowledge adds value and makes you feel important. On the surface, it appears that when you hoard, it's good, but when others hoard, it's bad! If you think you may be a hoarder yourself, remember too that being team-oriented is in, and hoarders are not seen as team players.

Summary

Are you a hoarder, a one-dimensional wonder, a political wolf, or an image manager? Are you so stupid that you don't even realize that you're a stupid one? (Didn't think so!) Before you answer these questions, consider that there are elements to each of these characters within each of us, and that's not a bad thing. A few examples: The fact that we're so concerned about image sets the bar higher for product quality. Our political skills help us understand the dynamics with our clients and prospects in the sales process. And so on. The problem starts when these "negatives" get in the way. And when they begin to unduly distract us, maybe then we should consider leaving the Mother Ship.

KEY POINTS

How closely do you identify with the challenges and opportunities typical of large organizations? If you leave the Mother Ship, you may not miss the bureaucracy, but you will miss your friends and colleagues who stay there. If you leave, you may also miss a steady income, job security, and the support systems that you currently take for granted. If you merely move to *another* Mother Ship, these comforting things will still be there. Unfortunately, so will the hoarders, the stupid ones, and the rest of the peanut gallery.

When the pros and cons of your large organization on balance become negative, consider what that means. Will the balance right itself, along with your frustration level? Or is it the beginning of a divide that will ultimately lead to your departure? No matter how the question of whether to go or stay is resolved, it doesn't hurt to at least consider the possibility of moving on – and the planning imperative that goes with it.

Chapter 3: Today's Business Environment

Every few years, the business environment settles into a "new normal," often caused by some sort of external event. During the last several years, we have seen significant change in both the technology and financial worlds. What did we learn? First, from the technology world:

- Speed to market matters, but there has to be a market that you're speeding to.
- Valuation by "eyeballs" is for the birds. Valuation by fundamentals is usually a better bet.
- A business plan has to be based on reality.
- Many arrogant "vice-presidents" of dot-com start-ups are back where they belong: earning their spurs the hard way, one step at a time.

And from the financial world:

- Businesses and consumers spend only when there is a real reason to.
- Diversification pays off. Most people look at their retirement savings (what's left of them) with gloom.
- It pays to be honest: Just ask those who ran Arthur Anderson, Enron, WorldCom, and many of the other companies tarnished by poor financial reporting ethics or fraud.

What do these lessons have to do with your decision to leave or stay? Simple: as George Santayana, the notable philosopher said, "Those who do not learn from history are doomed to repeat it." Consider where you might go next: How does the organization define its market? How is the organization valued? What is the business planning process, and how often is it reviewed? What is the experience of your future colleagues? And what is their track record and reputation in the marketplace?

Now answer these questions for your current employer. How do they stack up? And if you were a job candidate, would you take a position where you currently work? If your current employer doesn't do so well at this most basic level, it may be time to consider leaving.

Another change has been the steady erosion of employee loyalty. Consider all your colleagues. How many of them have worked their way up through the ranks, and how many have been hired from outside? If you looked at companies many years ago, there would be significantly fewer outside hires. This isn't surprising, considering that employees have primarily borne the impact of business environment changes. That you are still with your organization, and have been successful there over time, gives you a commodity that is becoming more valued as more employees lose it: loyalty.

After you've toed the company line for so long, will others see you as "bailing"?

While researching this book, there were several people who commented that the only loyalty they have is to their pay, and that everyone they know has moved, at least once, for more money. As we'll see later in the Job Quality Checklist, compensation is important, but it usually isn't the only reason people move – or the most important. At this point, suffice it to say that if you fundamentally don't like your job, money won't change your mind.

After a number of years being a leader within your organization, you may be troubled by thoughts of leaving. After you've toed the company line for so long, will others see you as "bailing"? And you certainly don't want to leave anyone in the lurch.

These feelings can be addressed by answering a few simple questions: If the company had to let you go, would the company be troubled with pangs of guilt? And when you had to do the last downsizing, did you rationalize your decisions as being "business, not personal"? If the company can feel this way about its employees, surely you can feel this way about the company.

There have been other environmental changes as well: September 11, and the fears of exported terrorism. On the health front, our new vocabulary includes mad cow disease, West Nile virus, and SARS. While these have all had a tragic impact on many individuals, geographic regions, and certain businesses, what impact might they have today, on you? Unlike the financial meltdowns discussed earlier, these other issues can be very personal. Would you have traveled to Beijing during the SARS scare? Do you still think twice about flying in and out of New York? And do you still believe that all beef is safe to eat? Important issues all, but however you feel about them is unlikely to affect your decision to stay or go. They may, however, affect your decision of where you *go to*.

KEY POINTS

- The changes in the last several years have taught us many valuable lessons. Some relate to basic business fundamentals (rather than eyeballs), others relate to the importance of honesty and disclosure in financial statements.
- The challenge is to learn from our environment, not just observe it.

Chapter 4: SkillChecks

It may have been some time since you've considered where your strengths are. Yes, you came into the business world in marketing, but over the last 10, 15, or 20 years, you have grown considerably. An inventory of both your hard and soft skills will help identify areas of weakness that require polishing, and areas of strength that might be leveraged as you move on.

Let's assume you are an accountant and are very good at what you do. You are thinking that your next step is not only out of the organization, but out of accounting as well. The purpose of an inventory or analysis is to help you identify the underlying skills (such as quantitative or analytical) that may be useful in a completely different venue. The analysis takes part in two sections. SkillCheck I requires you to write longhand answers to several questions, while SkillCheck II is a more traditional inventory. Try not to look at SkillCheck II until SkillCheck I is complete.

SkillCheck I

Write your answers longhand to the following six questions. Instead of using bullets, write from three to five paragraphs for each question. Writing longhand forces you to focus, without distraction, on each question. If you wish to type them into a computer, you can do so later.

1. What is your educational and training background? (Include university, professional certifications, internal and external seminars)
2. Look back at your college or university transcripts. Was there a course that you found interesting, but you never did follow up nor take more advanced training? Why was it interesting?
3. What specific skills did you hone to excellence in your previous three positions?
4. What aspects of your previous three positions were the most fun?
5. What areas of knowledge or skill do you see as your biggest weakness?

6. What non-work activities provide you the most satisfaction? What is it about these activities that interest you?

Most larger organizations force their staff to go through an annual appraisal process. You set your objectives, review performance against the previous objectives, and find out how much you'll be paid the next year. If you work for a progressive organization, you may even discuss your career objectives. But rarely will you be asked the questions in SkillCheck I, because there is little interest in information that is either very far away (educational training), or transcends several jobs over time. And if these questions are asked, for political reasons you might prefer not to be 100% honest with your answers. (That is, assuming you actually know your answers!)

The value of SkillCheck I is that it forces you to confront these questions directly. And in writing your answers, you have to spend time thinking.[3]

SkillCheck II

SkillCheck II is a ranking of your knowledge and skills[4] in a number of areas required in business. Needless to say, it does not "dive deep" but is designed to enumerate skills across a broad spectrum of knowledge. For each skill type, rank yourself according to the following criteria:

BASIC: Some training or knowledge in the area, but requires updating (or mentoring) to work independently.

INTERMEDIATE: Knowledgeable, but may have difficulty taking a leadership role in the area, or Guru, but slightly out of date.

GURU: Expert and leader in the area, publicly recognized.

BLANK: If you have no training or knowledge in the area (yet), leave the Self-Assessment column blank.

---

3. You may have had a similar experience the last time you updated your résumé.
4. We are using the terms "knowledge" and "skill" interchangeably, but of course they are different: knowledge refers to understanding, while skill refers to capability. For example, you may have significant knowledge about football, but your skills in it may be quite rusty.

Self Assessment: Basic/Intermediate/Guru	Marketing
________	Market Research
________	Product Development
________	Brand Strategy
________	Services Marketing
________	Direct Marketing
________	Internet Marketing
________	Channel Management
________	Corporate Identity
________	Media Relations/Public Relations
________	Government Relations
________	International Marketing
________	Database Marketing
________	Other ________
	Sales
________	Sales Management
________	Sales Forecasting
________	Sales (deals <100K)
________	Sales (deals between 100K and 1M)
________	Sales (deals >1M)
________	Pre-sales Support
________	Other ________
	Finance and Accounting
________	CFO
________	Corporate Finance - Banks and other lenders
________	Corporate Finance - Public markets/Regulatory issues
________	Treasury, Cash Management, Foreign Exchange
________	Accounting, Bookkeeping, Statement Preparation/Review
________	Activity-Based Costing
________	Financial Analysis
________	Mergers, Acquisitions, and Divestitures
________	Real Estate
________	Other ________
	MIS
________	Senior IT management (e.g., CIO or similar)
________	IT Program Management
________	Technical Architecture
________	Programming, Network, and System-Related Functions
________	Implementation of an ERP System
________	Implementation of a CRM System
________	Implementation of a Successful e-Commerce System
________	Other ________

Self Assessment: Basic/Intermediate/Guru	Manufacturing, Production, and Supply Chain
______	Factory Management
______	Quality Systems and Management
______	Logistics/Transportation
______	Import/Export
______	Purchasing
______	Inventory Management
______	Data Management
______	Other ______
	Human Resources
______	Most Senior HR Manager
______	HRIS Systems
______	Payroll Systems
______	Benefit and Pension Plans
______	HR Generalist
______	Corporate Trainer
______	Labor Negotiations
______	Other ______
	General Management and Miscellaneous
______	Turnarounds
______	Process Re-engineering
______	Project Management
______	Internal Consultant
______	Business Unit Head
______	Focus Group Facilitation
______	Board-level Experience
______	Legal Experience
______	Research and Development
______	Other ______
	Industry Vertical
______	Retail
______	Wholesale/Distributor
______	Manufacturer
______	Financial Services
______	Professional Services
______	Government/Public Services
______	Non-Government/Non-profit Organizations
______	Other ______

Note: All forms are available at www.LeavingTheMotherShip.com.

Okay, so you didn't actually do the two SkillChecks, did you? (Or maybe you just "scanned" them?) You want to get into the meat, and these exercises look like they would take a bit more time than you have right now. No problem. Just make sure that you actually do them, as the results will be used both to determine *when to go*, and later, as criteria for *where to go*. More reasons to do them now: SkillChecks help you better articulate your strengths to others and provide focus for how your time is spent until you leave.

SkillChecks help you better articulate your strengths to others.

SkillCheck I is "you-centered": across your career, what you are good at, where you are weak, and what you enjoy doing. The value of SkillCheck I is in the thinking and doing. SkillCheck II, which is a bit more mechanical, puts your skills in context with others: how well do you know what you know.

For those who completed the SkillChecks, the next task is analysis.

For those who did not do the SkillChecks at all, a stronger reminder: if you don't have the strength of mind to do simple exercises like the SkillChecks, how do you think you will survive after you've left the Mother Ship? You can't make change by passively reading a book – get yourself more fully engaged by actively going through these activities. Otherwise, you are missing an opportunity to develop discipline and strength of mind – key success factors after you leave.

ANALYZING SKILLCHECK I. Think through the areas that were easy to answer, and those that were more difficult. Spend a few moments considering why. Did some of your answers surprise you? You may find it useful to share your answers with your spouse or a close personal friend. Ask them if they see any surprises, or if they would have expected you to answer any of the questions differently.

ANALYZING SKILLCHECK II. Even though you may be uncertain where you will eventually land, it is important to acknowledge your blind spots (or "gaps"). As an example, suppose you are a lawyer, and you think you may be interested in biotech venture capital. A gap may exist if you have not yet developed skills in financial analysis or if you do not understand the biotech industry. If you are a CFO looking at general management but haven't had experience in sales or marketing, there may be a gap here too.

Review the results of SkillCheck II. A gap exists wherever you have left your self-assessment blank or rated your level as basic. Now ask yourself these questions about each gap:

- Are there gaps because you haven't ever been educated in the area before?
- Are there gaps because you have not yet had the opportunity to personally develop experience in the area? (Or because you've always shied away from trying?)
- Are there gaps because you really don't enjoy the area? (Or perhaps because you think that you wouldn't enjoy doing them?)

Part of determining the nature of any future training or education is to look at your basics and blanks, determine what is required for your next move, and then develop a plan to fill in the gaps. The problem, of course, is that you may not know what is required for your next move. So how do you *develop the plan to fill in the gaps*?

Use a proxy goal and plan toward that proxy.

The answer is simple: it doesn't matter if you don't know the exact place you're moving to; Part II of this book (Knowing Where to Go) should help with that. Use a proxy goal for now, and plan toward that proxy.[5] Once you've got a better idea of where you want to go, you can do a mid-course correction. When your goal is almost locked down, do yet another mid-course correction. And so on. The most important thing is not to do nothing: *do something that gets you approximately in the direction you want to go – and start doing it NOW!*

5. A proxy is a placeholder. For example, assume you were interested in finance, but weren't sure whether you were interested in corporate finance, mergers and acquisitions, or commercial banking. Choosing a proxy goal of corporate finance will allow you to plan in the general direction of finance; as you learn more, your proxy can become more specific, or it can change.

KEY POINTS

Developing the discipline to go through these exercises provides two major benefits: (1) you learn more about yourself, and (2) you develop the discipline that will be critical once you leave the Mother Ship.

ACTION CHECKLIST

- ❑ SkillCheck I
- ❑ SkillCheck II

Chapter 5: Job Quality Checklist

The Job Quality Checklist is an easy diagnostic tool that can help you determine whether it's time to make a job change or not. Answering yes or no to six easy questions gives you a barometer on the quality of your current position – and easy criteria for your next.

1. Are you still having fun?
2. Are you being challenged intellectually?
3. Do you like your colleagues?
4. Are you reaching your career goals?
5. Are you achieving life balance?
6. Is your compensation somewhat close to your worth?

While you might be able to think of one or two other important questions, answering these ones first should help you determine whether to leave or stay.

1. Still Having Fun?

When you wake up in the morning, are you actually excited about going into work, and looking forward to getting there? Or has work slowly become less and less fun?

If your attitude toward your job has changed, what was it that caused the change? Perhaps the chase was exciting, but now that you've arrived, you're not exactly thrilled with the destination. Or maybe a particular event has wakened you to your dissatisfaction.

I must admit that lying in the dentist's chair is not at all my idea of having fun. In fact, it is pretty much my least desired activity of all. Yet why do I go back, over and over through the years? Because my teeth are important, and it's worth the discomfort. If your job brings you no joy, better make sure the money is worth it.

Unless you enjoy each day, you are missing a significant part of life.

As easy as this question – "Still having fun?" – sounds, it is tough to answer honestly, as we often justify our answers after the fact. To start your thinking process, try answering the following five questions:

- If you could choose any job in the world, would it be the one that you're in right now?
- Do you get out of bed each morning, excited about going to the office?
- Do you find yourself arriving later than you did years before, and leaving earlier?
- Is the working atmosphere positive and exciting, or negative and gloomy?
- Ask your spouse and/or best friend: "Do you think that I am having fun at work? Am I excited about it? Do you think I would be happier elsewhere?"

Most people don't go to their jobs to have fun; some even rationalize this by saying that work and play are mutually exclusive activities. But unless you enjoy each day, you are missing a significant part of life.

For some jobs (nurses, firefighters, and funeral directors, for example), the concept of fulfillment seems more appropriate than the concept of fun. Each of these roles brings a high personal reward along that dimension. If you're in this type of job, and you think you've lost the spark, maybe it is no longer a fulfilling role for you. And maybe you're not having fun either.

2. Are You Being Challenged Intellectually?

We spend the first 18 years of our life sitting in school classrooms. We then spend a number of years in college or university; many of us pursue graduate degrees and professional certifications on top of that. Then we enter the workforce, and exchange our *learning* hat for an *earning* one. Why should the learning stop after school? Some professions (doctors and accountants, for example) require an annual number of professional development hours in order to remain certified. Enlightened organizations require all staff to participate in some sort of training each year.

But even if you attend training and professional development courses, it doesn't mean that your job itself provides intellectual challenge. In other words, do you have to use your head to do your job? For me, intellectual challenge means that I must always be learning. Others find intellectual challenge by being exposed to new and constantly changing technology. For you, the intellectual challenge must be...appropriate for you.

Intellectual challenge gives you the flexibility to deal with change.

While intellectual challenge may not be such a high priority for everyone, a job that provides continuous intellectual challenge keeps you interested in the day-to-day. It also prevents you from "growing dumb" over the years.

More importantly, though, is that intellectual challenge gives you the flexibility to deal with change. And if you are thinking of leaving the Mother Ship, you *will need* that flexibility.

3. Do You Like Your Colleagues?

When you pick your friends, you pretty much have complete latitude. If you don't like someone (or they don't like you), you just don't spend time together. In the workplace, it's not so simple: you're thrown together and must work to meet common objectives.

Work is a lot more pleasant when you enjoy working with your colleagues. It is a lot easier to get things done when you have a positive relationship with your manager, co-workers, and staff. It reduces the negative politics considerably and, when you're in a bind, gives you people to call upon.

"Do you like your colleagues?" doesn't mean that you have to be close personal friends. Nor does it mean that you have to be strong political allies. And it certainly doesn't mean currying favor with others so *they* like *you*. It means that you have a generally positive attitude to them, and enjoy your interactions with them when you are with them in a business setting.

Interestingly, as you spend more and more time together, you will start taking on some of your colleagues' attributes, and they yours. Didn't like how rude everyone was when you started your job? Look in the mirror several years later: you have probably become ruder too!

If you answered "Of course I like my colleagues," try these two litmus test questions:

If you have enough experience for a senior role outside, you have enough experience for a senior role where you are now.

- Would I leave my children with them for a week?
- What would my mother say about my colleagues?

If you don't like your answers to these two questions, maybe you don't like your colleagues as much as you thought. It is a plain fact that it is easier to work with people you like than those you don't. And if you don't like the people that you work with…maybe it is time to leave the Mother Ship!

Now, try substituting the word "boss" for colleague. Your boss can clear the way for you politically and improve your standing in the organization; a boss's word can result in promotion and better compensation. A good boss can act as a mentor or coach.

What happens if you have a bad boss? Should you leave or should you stay? Surely if you are beginning to despise your time at work, you might consider a change. But does the change mean leaving altogether, or merely moving to another position within the organization?

You might think that staying in your current position is necessary for consideration for a more senior role. If this is the case, ask yourself if you now have an adequate amount of experience for that same senior role in another organization. If you do, don't delude yourself about the necessity of staying. If you have enough experience for a senior role outside, you have enough experience for a senior role where you are now.

Why suffer with a boss you don't like? At least consider moving on.

4. Are You Reaching Your Career Goals?

Your company has many stakeholders, including shareholders, customers, suppliers, employees, and perhaps also the general public. As it tries to satisfy all these groups, it is pretty much impossible to hit a "bull's eye" each time and for each group. For employees, bonus plans, objective-setting, and stock options can generate some degree of alignment. But with the exception of sole proprietorships and closely held partnerships, an organization's goals are rarely 100% aligned with those of any one particular individual.

Given this reality, how do you assess whether your current job is heading *you* toward *your* goals?

Think of your career plan as a wide arrow, going in a particular direction. Then think of a particular trajectory within that arrow: that is the direction your current job is taking you.

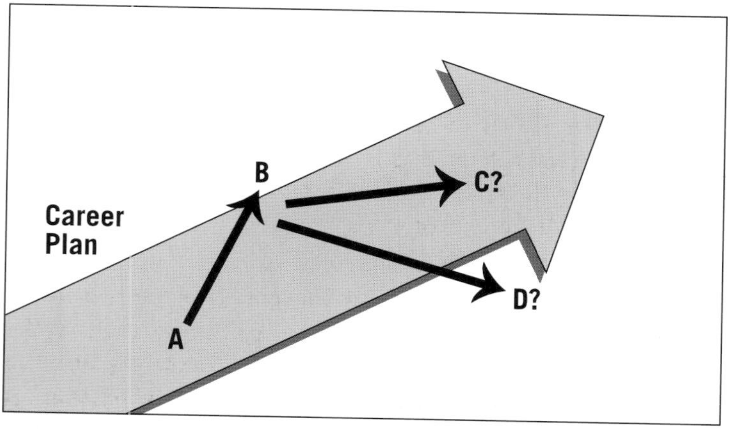

The diagram shows you at point A – the start of your last "job" within the organization. At point B, your current job is about to conflict with your desired career path. Perhaps you are in a staff position but feel that you should be in a line position. In any case, if you keep on the same path, you would not be in alignment and would eventually become frustrated. If you were to take job B, one of your considerations should be whether this new job takes you to point C or D. The greater the alignment, the faster you achieve your goals, and more likely, the greater your satisfaction.

At point B, however, you can make another decision. You may wish to re-evaluate your career plan and re-orient it to be in the direction of your current job. In this case, neither C nor D would make any sense, and you should look around for a position like one at point E – maybe even outside the organization.

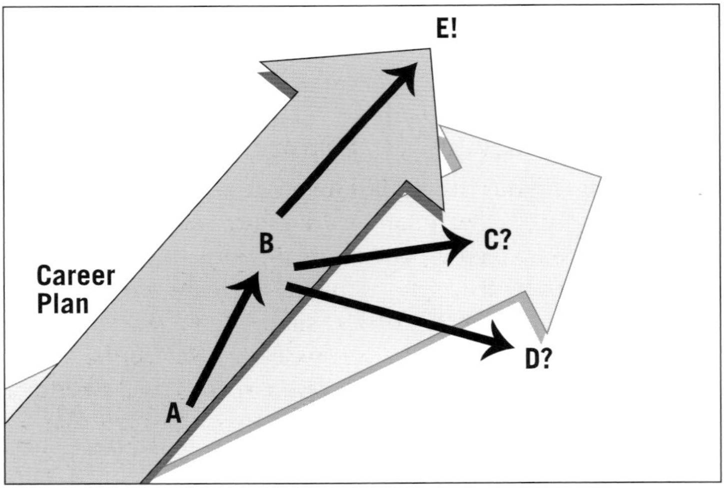

Here's an example. Assume that you have been recently appointed as the manager in charge of receivables in a corporation's finance department. Ever since you joined the company years ago as a junior accountant, your goal has been to become the treasurer; in fact, that is likely the next step for you. Meanwhile, another job opportunity comes up, running the finance department for a subsidiary of the company. Should you take it? If you do, you won't get the experience necessary for the treasurer's job. But on the other hand, running an entire department sounds fascinating and might mean even greater opportunity in the future. The decision is about a job – but also about your direction.

Remember that your career, and the jobs you take within it, are based on decisions that are yours to make. It doesn't matter whether you keep your career direction the same (e.g., job C or D), or choose to re-orient your career direction (and therefore take job E), so long as the choice you make is one that is made deliberately. Be careful, though, that you don't justify a career direction change just to fit a convenient job at your current employer.

Don't justify a career direction change just to fit a convenient job at your current employer.

If your job is taking you outside your career plan direction, and you're unwilling to change your career direction for the organization's sake, consider the possibility that your next job may be elsewhere.

5. Are You Achieving Life Balance?

Reflecting on our accomplishments and successes, we can often attribute it to our strong work ethic: never saying no to new responsibility; going the extra mile for that important customer; working through the night to get the proposal just right. However, for many of us, success has meant certain compromises along the way. Excessive travel. Neglecting fitness and health. Having no time for hobbies or volunteer activities. Spending little time with your family – if you still have one.

At different times in your life, there may be different priorities, and at the beginning of your career, your first priority is likely to be… your career. However, after this initial push to establish yourself, there should be a movement toward balance; without it, you will pay a steep price, often in ways you could never foresee.

A former colleague of mine was known to be able to "fix" just about any project that had gone off the rails. He had fun on each of his assignments, and he did find them challenging. He was working with people he liked, and each assignment raised his profile in the company. He certainly was paid well enough. Unfortunately, each assignment also had one other thing in common: it took about 18 hours each day, six days a week, for about three months. As one can expect, this schedule didn't leave time for much else. After many years of working like this, he realized he had missed much of his children's formative years – a steep price indeed, paid by him and his children. He also paid an ugly price with his health, having to take stress leave several times along the way.

While this is only one example, what are the other typical costs of not having balance? How about teenager problems, celibacy in marriage, divorce, ulcers, eating disorders, obesity, heart attacks, and nervous breakdowns? Not a pretty list!

Here's another way to look at the question of balance: what is the price you have already paid for your business success so far, and what is the price you are willing to pay in the future? If the price sounds a bit steep, you already know the answer to this question. Chapter 8 introduces the concept of the Personal Balance Sheet, a tool that can help you assess, then achieve, a better life balance.

6. Is Your Compensation Somewhat Close to Your Worth?

It has always amazed me how poorly compensation plans are conceived and executed; how certain plans are too rich or too poor; how plans consistently reward the external job hoppers and penalize the internal rising stars. I'm also amazed at the simplistic mechanisms that are used to tie pay to performance. Very few of us honestly believe that we're paid too much for the work we do; most of us believe we are under-compensated. So given all this unfairness, how do we pin down exactly what we're worth? The answer is that we can't. The correct question is simply "Are we paid somewhat close to our 'worth'?"

To answer that question, answer these:

- Do you have enough income to provide for life's necessities?
- Is your compensation plan plus or minus 15% of others doing comparable jobs within the organization?

- Have you been approached by a recruiter *for the same job at a comparable employer,* with a compensation plan within 15% of your current plan?
- If the organization replaced you, how much would they have to pay?
- Based on available salary surveys, are you in the bottom quartile of pay, yet are a recognized star performer within your organization?

This "compensation" attribute should be in the Job Quality Checklist, but should only be looked at last. If you're paid a bit too little, think of it as an investment in your managerial training. If you're paid too much, perhaps it is to make up for a deficiency in the other attributes. In any case, the compensation plan shouldn't be the primary driver for your decision to leave – the other attributes are.

KEY POINTS

How do you know when to leave? The Job Quality Checklist provides the fundamental criteria. If these six attributes (Fun, Challenge, Like your colleagues, Goals, Balance, Compensation) are all at an acceptable level, perhaps you shouldn't leave the Mother Ship – at least for now. If you don't like enough of your answers, maybe it's time to go.

ACTION CHECKLIST

❑ Job Quality Checklist

Chapter 6:
Maybe You Should Still Stay...for a While

If several of the six attributes in the Job Quality Checklist are negative, this is a clear indicator that you should consider leaving. What isn't clear, though, is the question of when. There are several *bona fide* reasons to stick around, at least temporarily:

- It may take some time to put your financial house in order; an expected bonus or stock option may be date-bound. Or you may wish to accumulate more money before taking the next step.
- It may take a period of time for you to determine what exactly *should* be your next step.
- You might want to spend some time filling in the gaps (see the next section of this book). Doing this on your current employer's tab is *very* cost-effective!

Make sure that your Very Good Reason is indeed a good reason and not an excuse to keep with the status quo.

It is too easy to convince yourself to stay, notwithstanding all the ideas we've reviewed. There is always a very good reason! Just make sure that your Very Good Reason is indeed a good reason and not an excuse to keep with the status quo. Here are a few reasons for not leaving that might resonate, and a counterpoint to get you thinking:

- Perhaps some of the negatives in your current situation are only temporary. *But* ask yourself whether they will self-correct over the next six months. And for how long has "temporary" been underway so far?
- Perhaps you are paid so much money that you are willing to stay and "take your lumps." *But* ask yourself how long you are willing to put up with the negatives before these negatives start doing you real harm – especially off the job.
- Perhaps you work for a family business, and you are required to "prove yourself" for a period of time before being given real responsibility (and possibly ownership). *But* ask yourself whether this time period is likely to be extended, and whether external experience might be even more highly valued. And ask yourself if the succession plan is known to others beside yourself.

- Perhaps the job gives you something else that you value even more highly, such as flexibility for family time, life insurance, or health care coverage that you couldn't get elsewhere. These are all very good reasons to stay, assuming you are right. *But* are you really 100% sure you couldn't find family flexibility with another employer? Or life and health insurance as good or better? Don't assume! If you don't look, you'll never really know.

If you're still intent on staying, it doesn't mean that you shouldn't plan!

Despite all this, if you're still intent on staying, keep reading anyway – it doesn't mean that you shouldn't learn and plan!

Timeframe and Commitments

Many years ago, loyalty between employer and employee was the rule. For most organizations, the necessity of economics has meant a very real deterioration of that loyalty. As an example, compare the average number of years service ten years ago in your organization to the same statistic of today. Consider the number of cuts you have had to make, for the "good of the organization." If an employer can make its staffing decisions based solely on its needs, then surely you have the same right to do so for yourself. Don't let misplaced loyalty or comfort detract you from doing the analysis and making your personal career decisions.

After reviewing hundreds of résumés, I found that some always stuck out as "job hoppers." While these people's experience often looked relevant, it was hard not to think of them as opportunists, always looking out for themselves first, and their employers second.

Several years ago, I hired one of these people. He was an impressive individual who even came with a personal recommendation from a trusted employee. Unfortunately, this person's on-the-job behavior was all too predictable. He was very good with clients, he was aggressive, and he was technically competent. But he had the annoying habit of constantly referring to his experience at one of his many previous jobs. Before the year was out, he quit for another Exciting Opportunity, adding my company's name to his ever-growing résumé. The grass is always greener indeed!

Whether you believe the above example to be an outlier or typical, a résumé that shows promotion within an organization provides proof of your added value and your loyalty.

A résumé that shows promotion within an organization provides proof of your added value and your loyalty.

But how often should you consider staying or leaving the organization? One of my first managers had an interesting approach. He would commit to a particular position for two years, and then review his goals at that time. If it turned out that his goals were being met, he would re-commit for another two years. If not, he would aim for a job change (either internally or externally) by the end of the third year. Whether you commit to the two years publicly or just to yourself, the key is that you are making a commitment to be singularly focused for a specific time period. You are loyal, but only insofar as your current job is in alignment with your career plan.

A benefit of this approach is that you avoid hurting your long-term interests, by focusing on the task at hand: your current job. Once you have made the decision to leave, however, you have two jobs: your *day job* working for your employer, and your *night job* preparing for the next step away.

KEY POINTS

- We never hesitate to find justifications that prevent us from doing what we must. Sometimes, these justifications become so comfortable that we see them as truth. We construct reasons to stay that seem reasonable, but when stripped bare, aren't real reasons at all.
- Commit to your job in two-year increments.
- Once you decide to leave, recognize that you really have two jobs: the *day job* that pays the bills now, and the *night job* that will pay the bills in the future.

Chapter 7: Triggering Events

Olympic sprinters spend a lot of time training. Weights, endurance, stretching, and practice are all part of their daily regime. When they get a telephone call from their coach confirming the date of a race, their regime quickly changes to one of preparation for that day. The telephone call is a triggering event. At the starting line, when the starting pistol goes off, the sprinter goes into action, racing as quickly as possible. Again, the starting pistol is a triggering event: it changes the runner's state of mind from anticipation to action.

What will cause you to finally say that it's time to leave the Mother Ship *now?*

In this chapter, we'll look at some triggering events for you. What will cause you to finally say that it's time to leave the Mother Ship *now?* Maybe it's when you finally set your own goals; maybe it's when you're fed up and think that you could do better. Maybe it's when all of your planning comes together, or when you are shocked into action by an unexpected life event. And maybe you just happen to catch a lucky break. Whatever it is in the end, understanding what a starting pistol is used for is the first step in starting the race properly – or at all.

Keeping Up with the Joneses

Competition and comparison can be very powerful allies. You compare yourself with others in your graduating class, and push harder so that you don't fall behind. You compete with friends, siblings, and maybe even your spouse, to see who can make the most money, have the most prestigious title, and garner the best perks. More so than pressure from a manager, competition can push you to achieve far more than you ever thought possible. You keep up with the Joneses.

The more money you earn, the more you spend. The more you spend, the more you have to earn. When this cycle is also fuelled by keeping up with the Joneses, the dual problems of job velocity and life velocity intersect. What was once merely a question of showing neighbors that we are keeping up has changed into something that causes our life balance to be seriously eroded.

There is a more subtle cost to keeping up with the Joneses: you are implicitly measuring yourself against others' goals, not your own. When you began your career, this wasn't a big issue; so long as you were climbing up the corporate ladder, everything was okay. But as you began to achieve real success, you started to recognize that your career goals and others' career goals were not the same. (You also probably realized that buying things doesn't bring enduring happiness.)

Measure yourself against your goals, not others!

Many young men and women go into the same business or profession as their parents, whisked there with strong parental expectations or pressure. Again, after a certain point in time, they may have the same recognition: their career goals and their parents' goals are not the same.

How to know when it is time to go? When you realize that you are in charge of setting your goals, and yet your current path is someone else's. Consider leaving when others' expectations are no longer as important as your own; when it is no longer important to be keeping up with the Joneses.

Fed Up, and Think You Can Do Better

Working for a larger organization, you probably have seen plenty of really dumb decisions. Sometimes these are made because of politics, sometimes ignorance or ego, and sometimes because of poor business acumen.

As part of a mature management team, you may debate, argue, and cajole privately as much as you like, but once the decision is made, it is expected that you will support the decision as if it were your own. Most of these decisions, when outside your direct area of responsibility, you can live with, even if you think they are misguided. Some of the decisions that affect your scope, you will swallow like a bitter pill, for the good of the organization. Team player!

The more you swallow, though, the more fed up you will be. In fact, there comes a point when you recognize a fundamental difference in the way your employer operates and the way you would operate. The impact could be along any number of different dimensions: in customer service, employee morale, product development, financial reporting, or sales.

If you really think you can do better, maybe it's time to consider going.

Especially when these differences mount, it is frustrating to put on your team face and promote what you see as misguided decisions. Why keep swimming upstream? If you really think you can do better, maybe it's time to consider going.

You Have a Plan and Want to Launch

Over the last few years, you and a few of your old college classmates have been beavering away at a new business idea, dedicating nights and weekends to getting ready. Now is the time, and you jump: you are practically assured of success, as all things have been perfectly planned so that nothing is left to chance!

This unlikely scenario is marred by a few realities. Psychologically, it is hard to actually quit your job and jump, no matter how well you've planned. Usually this is because you have thought so much *about* the business, but not the transition *to* the business. Your plan likely doesn't include launch criteria (or more specifically, it doesn't include any "quitting your day job" criteria).

If you are currently functioning in this mode, you can use the following criteria to frame your timing decision. It is time to leave...

- ...when there is a conflict (of time or of interest) between your day job and your new enterprise.
- ...when your marketing materials are mostly complete, and you can actually start selling.
- ...after you've made your first commitment to a supplier.
- ...when you are able to start approaching sources of funding with your business plan. (They'll want to see you 100% committed anyway.)

- ... if you suddenly may be able to take advantage of a severance offer.
- ...if it looks like the competitive window for the success of your business idea is starting to close. *Leave real fast!*
- ...when you have accepted a written offer of employment for another position.

Especially if you have partners, you should all agree on these criteria, even if they are different for each of you. Harmonizing expectations will significantly reduce problems later on.

Extended planning has a number of benefits, but one of the most important is helping you re-cast your self-image into your new role. The more you feel comfortable, the more confident you will be. Furthermore, if you're changing industries or doing something you haven't done before, research and planning can mitigate personal risk. On the other hand, if you see a real opportunity and don't jump at it ("Damn the torpedoes, full steam ahead!"), you'll be kicking yourself for years.

Watch out for planning paralysis. If you've done even half of what you think is necessary, maybe it's time to get going.

Watch out for planning paralysis. If you've done even half of what you think is necessary, maybe it's time to get going. Large corporation life has given you comfort doing huge planning exercises – especially if you are going to be an entrepreneur, you must practice being agile. And the agility practice should start at the planning stage, since agility will not magically appear after you've launched.

You Get a Kick in the Head

What got you started thinking about leaving the Mother Ship in the first place? Often, we go through life, ticking off achieved objectives one by one, and then something happens that wakes us up.

One day, leaving the office, I stopped to say goodbye to my manager. He was in his mid to late 50s, brilliant, and full of energy and ideas. That day, he looked completely ashen. He had just learned of a colleague's sudden heart attack and death. The heart attack victim was his age. While he was certainly sad about losing a friend, this was the first of his generation to pass away, and he recognized that it could easily have been he who had the heart attack. This was a kick in the head. Although he is now well into his 60s and still working, he exercises each day and is far healthier than he was at that time. Guess why.

What other types of *kicks* are there? A personal medical crisis. A family member diagnosed with a terminal disease. The birth of your first child, or death of a parent. Maybe your spouse wants a divorce. Perhaps someone "untouchable" gets fired. Or maybe you get passed over for promotion.

Whatever it is, good or bad, the event effectively jolts you out of your complacency and causes you to think differently, perhaps for the first time in years.

The Bluebird Principle

A bluebird is an opportunity. It flies in the window, sings its beautiful song ("Make money and have fun"), and waits for you to do the one thing required for it to take flight. Unfortunately, human nature is what it is; although we recognize the opportunity, we often don't believe it when we see it. Perhaps this is laziness, perhaps it is pride; whatever the reason, we let the opportunity fly away.

When I started giving my children an allowance, I made a deal with them: if they practiced piano each and every day, at the end of the week I would double their allowance. Care to guess how rarely the payout was made? The Bluebird Principle starts at a very young age!

We aren't always afflicted with this laziness; sometimes we grab the Bluebird and we reap the rewards. Perhaps we have successful careers because we feel comfortable grabbing the Bluebird at work. When it is for our own account, though, it seems much, much tougher indeed.

If we are leaving, what are some examples of Bluebirds? A colleague mentions, "If only we could find a product that did XYZ" – and you know exactly where to find such a product.

A friend wants you to personally bid on an exciting project at their company – and you know how to do the project at lowest cost. While on vacation overseas you see a tremendous concept – and you know exactly how to bring it to market domestically.

If you don't jump up and grab it, the Bluebird will fly away.

Each of these examples has one thing in common: if you don't jump up and grab it, the Bluebird will fly away. The window of opportunity closes at the end of the proverbial day.

So how can you avoid the Bluebird Principle? This is a bit like asking the question about how to avoid procrastination and laziness! Make your decision to leave, make your decision on where you should go, continue with your planning, and then act. If a Bluebird disrupts those plans, then don't let process get in the way. Grab the Bluebird and fly.

Knowing When to Go: Final Thoughts

How strongly you identify with many of the issues described here depends on your experience. At this point, at least in your mind, you should be making progress toward leaving the Mother Ship:

- You have a decent written inventory of your skills and experience.
- You understand – through the Job Quality Checklist – how good (or bad) your current position is.
- You may have a tighter understanding of your timelines.
- While you may not know exactly when you will go, you recognize there are some things that should be done before you leave, both personally and professionally.

Even if you decide that leaving in the near future is not for you, it still doesn't hurt to plan. And in the meantime, look out for those triggering events.

KEY POINTS

- Look out for Bluebirds and Triggers.
- Stay away from the Joneses: define your own goals instead of using others'.
- If you get kicked in the head, use it as a catalyst for action. Particularly if the kick is painful, avoid emotional paralysis by focusing on moving forward.

PART II:

Knowing Where to Go

Now might be an opportune time to consider the name of this book: ***Leaving the Mother Ship.*** *Consider: what type of Mother Ship are you on right now? Is it a speedboat, aircraft carrier, or luxury cruise ship? While I'm sure no one will admit to being on the* Titanic, *some days it may feel like it!*

You may define yourself as being in financial services, technology, and management, working for a 20,000-employee organization, in a branch environment. While I can't tell if this is an aircraft carrier or the *Queen Mary*, the dynamics are surely different than if you were a senior civil servant working in liaison with the defence industry. If you function extremely well on an aircraft carrier, imagine how different your professional life would be on a speedboat – or on a different aircraft carrier, or on the *Queen Mary*.

Part I of this book was designed to fuel your tanks and start your engine. But inertia without direction won't bring results. *Knowing where to go* will help you with direction and will help you distinguish between all the different "ships" available.

We'll start with career planning in context, but from first principles: how do you define success? We'll then look at how others have achieved success, and see what lessons can be drawn for you. We'll look at the options, including some you may not have seriously considered before, and then look at the criteria for choosing.

Once you've chosen, you will have your basic direction; it then becomes infinitely clearer how to use your time between now and when you leave. And finally, we'll give you a few practical suggestions for when you actually do the jump.

Chapter 8: Career Planning in Context

Depending upon who you talk to, the purpose of career planning can be defined in many ways:

- How to continuously get promoted to higher-paying jobs.
- How to "take charge" of your career by switching from company to company in search of higher-paying jobs.
- How to plan your career holistically, with training and education, to let you qualify for higher-paying jobs.
- How to do a job search, to leave your low-paying job and get that higher-paying job.

While the goal of looking for a higher-paying job is extremely important, most people have a few other motivations as well: fun, intellectual challenge, whether you like your colleagues, to name a few. (Sound familiar? Remember the Job Quality Checklist?)

We're going to look at career planning through a different lens: Does your *career* head you toward your *personal* goals? We'll do this by helping you define, for yourself, what success actually means.

Personal Balance Sheet

"Of course I'm successful – look at my car!"

Not surprisingly, defining success generically is pretty much impossible, as each person has a uniquely personal view of success itself. The Personal Balance Sheet is a productive model to use, as it defines the categories in which success may be found: Community, Family, Intellectual, Spiritual, Physical, Career, and Financial. Consider what each of these mean, and answer some of the following questions:

COMMUNITY: What is your community profile? Do you know your neighbors? What have you contributed to the community you live in? Are you making an impact there? Do others recognize your contribution? Are you satisfied with the friendships you have outside the workplace? Do you care about where you live at all?

FAMILY: How good are your family relationships? Do you ever experience guilt over how much (or how little) time you spend with your family? How close is your extended family? Are you making a positive impact on the lives of your children, spouse, and parents? Do you have a spouse? Is your relationship growing closer, or is it heading toward divorce? Is family relevant to you at all?

INTELLECTUAL: Are you getting smarter, or are you getting "dumber" each year? How many challenging non-fiction books do you read each year, outside of work-related titles? Can you still do complex math in your head, or do you routinely look for a calculator or spreadsheet first?

SPIRITUAL: Do you regularly spend time contemplating spiritual ideas? Are you involved in any religious learning? Do you feel comfortable answering your children's questions about religion and spirituality? Do you feel guilty about not spending enough time in this area? Is spirituality relevant at all to you?

PHYSICAL: Do you think you could be in better shape? Are you unhappy or embarrassed with the way your body looks? Do you feel unhealthy? Does your doctor give you health advice (stop smoking, start jogging, lose weight, eat properly) that you don't follow to the letter? Is physical health relevant to you at all?

FINANCIAL: Do you think you are compensated appropriately, given your job and your efforts? Are you making as much money as you had expected to? Do you own your own house, car, boat, etc.? Do you worry about your level of debt? Are you saving enough for the future (e.g., retirement, children's education, house)?

CAREER: Has your career progressed to where you expected it to be by now? Do you feel you are in control of your career? If you had to do it all over again, would you have taken a different direction, or done something else?

If asked publicly, most people would say that they are successful, and might justify their success by pointing to their car, home, or job title. Privately though, I doubt many people are as happy as they want to be. Remember: the point of career planning is to ensure that your *career* helps you achieve your *personal* goals, not the other way around. The following exercise helps determine if this has been the case with you.

Career planning ensures that your *career* helps you achieve your *personal* goals, not the other way around.

PERSONAL BALANCE SHEET: Before we even start, go through the questions above and write down your answers, even if it is in the margins of this book. (This exercise is more helpful if you are brutally honest with yourself!)

Think back to the beginning of your career – if you can remember that far back. What were your aspirations? Even if they were somewhat naive, those goals eventually led you to where you are today. Then think about the goals you had five years ago. Had your aspirations changed from when you started out? Likely they had, given the benefit of your experience. Write these all down in the first two columns in the chart below.

Now, consider your "current status," and use the answers to the earlier questions to fill in the *current status* column. And finally, write down your next goal on the chart, before you move on. It is not critical to have your next goals locked down tight at this stage; you can always make changes later. Leave the last column (with the diamond) blank.

Depending on your honesty, some of the Personal Balance Sheet may be very hard to fill out. If so, it is worthwhile asking yourself why. Had you not thought along these dimensions

Personal Balance Sheet

Dimension of Success	Goal at start of career	Goal five years ago	Current status (answers to questions)	Your next "goal"	◆
Community					
Family					
Intellectual					
Spiritual					
Physical					
Financial					
Career					

before? Or had your career planning and goal setting always been done in the context of your current employer, rather than in the context of "you"? Clarifying your next goal along these dimensions gives you a starting point for action.

At different points of your life, your priorities will change.

Defining success is very personal. For example, some people may weigh Career and Financial as extremely high, to the exclusion of all other attributes; other people may rate Family or Spiritual highest. It is also important to realize that at different points of your life, your priorities will change.

In Part I of this book, we briefly spent time on the importance of balance, but in the context of whether your current job allows you to have it. Now, after a fuller exploration, success can be defined simply as achieving *your* desired balance. But how do you know what the future impact of today's "balance" choices might be? Sometimes it's tough to see the forest for the trees, and an outside perspective can help. One of the best ways to do this is to go through a simple yet powerful exercise, called Reality Check Interviews.

Reality Check Interviews

Reality Check Interviews look at success from a different perspective: someone else's. What would the impact be of a different mix of priorities? We know about ourselves, because we live in our bodies and experience the impact of our decisions each and every day. But how have other people made similar decisions, as they chased their own success? And those decisions – have they paid off? What can you learn from their experience, and what advice might they give to you, if asked? Reality Check Interviews are called that because they are grounded in the real experiences of others.

The first step is to make a list of 30 people whom you see as being successful. These people, hopefully all with more years of experience than you, will have arrived at their current station in life through one path or another. They can be entrepreneurs, corporate executives, politicians, clergy, publishers, or anyone whom you believe has a story to tell. Do not seek only those who know you well for this exercise. Those who know you only peripherally (or not at all) may have had a unique career path, and their perspective could be important to you. It may be tempting to interview only 10 to 15 people, but push yourself for all 30. While finding 30 may be difficult, forcing this number ensures that the list goes beyond "the usual suspects," and that there is an appropriate variety of experience to review.

The overall objective is to individually interview these people – for 30 minutes, 45 at the most – and ask them a series of questions that help you understand how they got to where they are now. A secondary objective is to ask them for feedback about you.

Process

- Explain the purpose of the meeting. You're approaching a turning point in your career, and you're meeting several senior people whom you see as successful; you'd like to understand how they got to where they did, and some of the reasons behind the choices they made. You wanted to take 30 minutes, 45 at the most, etc., etc.
- I have found that interviewing the person for breakfast or lunch works better than meeting at their office, where distractions can cut the meeting short. (In case you had any other ideas: if you meet over a meal, don't be cheap – pick up the tab!)
- Don't ever tack this interview onto another reason for meeting. And don't bring anyone else to the meeting with you!
- When you meet with them, let them know that the conversation is private and confidential; ask if it is okay to take notes. It may help to imagine yourself as a newspaper writer, dispassionately collecting facts for an article.
- After the interview, summarize your notes into a "meeting memo" for later reference.
- Send a thank you note.

Here is a list of questions to get you started. Note that the questions go from the general to the private. As people get more comfortable talking about themselves, they will reveal more sensitive (and therefore more valuable) information to you.

- Can you give me a rundown on your career?
- Did you get any "big breaks," or was there a specific turning point? Elaborate on the impact…
- Did you create any of these big breaks yourself? Elaborate on how…
- What was the best piece of advice your mentors gave you?
- If you could go back and re-do some of your decisions, what would they be?
- Were there any unexpected trade-offs that happened as a result of your success? (e.g., personal relationships, less community involvement)
- How active are you in non-work activities – personal fitness, church, education, etc.?
- How would you define "success," generally? What grade (e.g., A-B-C-D-F) would you give yourself on the success scale?
- If you could rewind the clock, was there one thing you could have done that would have improved your grade?

Halfway through the meeting, change the focus from them to you. The questions you ask are determined by your relationship with them. For example, if someone knows you as a volunteer, their feedback will be through that lens. If they know you as a former workmate, their feedback will reflect their workplace experience with you. Of course, the better they know you, the more relevant their response. If they don't know you at all, modify the questions appropriately. Here are several of the "me" questions to get you started.

- You've known me in the capacity of _______; if you could put a label on my greatest strength, what would it be?
- What would you say my "blind side" was?

- Five years in the future, what type of business would you see me running/what type of role would you see me playing?
- What might you see as my first step in getting there?

These interviews are not designed to be "information interviews" of the sort used in job searches; they are to help you mature your own understanding of success.

Findings

While the results of each interview will be unique, there will be some common threads:

- You will begin to identify positively with some of the things that are said. You will also identify some of the problems you should avoid.
- People may lament that the cost of their success has been very high; often spoiled personal relationships, for example. Think through how each interviewee would have filled out their own Personal Balance Sheet.
- After 20-odd interviews, many of the responses will start to sound familiar. As this starts to happen, you should begin feeling that your "direction" – Knowing Where to Go – is becoming less nebulous.

When you have completed all the Reality Check Interviews, spend time summarizing your meeting notes. What were the common attributes, positive and negative? What lessons have you drawn from these successful people?

Finally, close the loop by going back to your Personal Balance Sheet. Make two changes:

1. **REVIEW YOUR CURRENT GOALS.** Do they still make sense to you, given what you've learned in the Reality Check Interviews? You may want to refine and possibly modify them as a result. Make sure your goals are both practical and attainable within the next 12 to 18 months.

2. **ADD ANOTHER COLUMN, ENTITLED CRITERIA FOR SUCCESS.** In the Personal Balance Sheet, there is a blank column headed by a diamond. Based on what you've learned, how do you now define success for each dimension? These should be longer-term criteria. Answer the question: "I'll know I am successful in my [family, financial, etc.] life when ________".

How can you tell whether you are (or are becoming) a one-dimensional wonder?

Defining Yourself in Terms of Your Job

Now that you have completed your Personal Balance Sheet and have better clarity on *your* definition of success, it is time to revisit one of the frustrations we described in Part I of this book: the *one-dimensional wonder*. This is the worker who is solely focused on work, to the exclusion of everything else. Even though the Reality Check Interviews and the Personal Balance Sheet may have softened you a bit, how can you tell whether you are (or are becoming) a one-dimensional wonder?

As an experiment, when you next go out with non-work friends, count how many times you bring up a work-related topic. And how many times your friends do so. A tougher test: how many times during a social occasion do you have work-related issues on your mind? And when you meet someone for the first time, how do you introduce yourself: as "a banker with XYZ"… or by a non-work trait?

When you define yourself solely on the basis of your job, and your job disappears, there is a problem: your self-image often disappears too. This predicament, usually felt by people who are fired, is also a problem when you leave the Mother Ship voluntarily. You no longer will have the comfort of saying that you are a banker with XYZ. To reduce this impact, get into the habit *now* of introducing yourself socially without mentioning your work. How? Here's a hint: describe yourself in terms of the other dimensions of success. At the start, try to memorize this description.

KEY POINTS

- Career planning traditionally is done within the box of possibilities available in your organization. This is wrong. Your career should lead you toward your personal goals. Your job shouldn't define who you are as a person.
- Success is defined very personally along a number of dimensions: Community, Family, Intellectual, Spiritual, Physical, Financial, and Career.

ACTION CHECKLIST

- ❑ Personal Balance Sheet
- ❑ Reality Check Interviews

Chapter 9: Looking at the Options

There are many different organizational formats, roles, and business possibilities. We will go over some of the more common options, along with the pros and cons of each.

Many of us have a natural tendency to dismiss unfamiliar or uncomfortable options. As you read, ask yourself, why couldn't I do this? As you manufacture reasons for not doing a particular item, manufacture other reasons why you can. Avoid closing the door on *any* idea.

Start-Up/Entrepreneur

Is there a way for you to "test-drive" the business beforehand?

Becoming an entrepreneur is one of the most challenging alternatives, but also the most satisfying when success finally comes. You will be competing against established organizations that have customer relationships, supplier deals in place, brand equity, and likely a stronger financial base. On the other hand, your start-up might not have the overheads or the "old technology" that constrain your entrenched competitors. Your new perspective and out-of-the-box thinking might be able to change the rules of the game, giving you a sustainable competitive advantage.

A start-up is special from another perspective as well. Everything is new. There are no established processes, policies, or procedures. There are no "HR departments," succession-planning issues, or 25-year long-service awards. While you may enjoy the title of president, unwittingly you will also have the title of janitor, secretary, messenger, purchasing clerk, and anything else that is not directly someone else's responsibility. Developing a start-up operation is sometimes described as giving birth to a vision.

If the business is in an area that is not known to you, what can be done to reduce your risks? And is there a way for you to "test-drive" the business beforehand? The answer to both these questions is *yes*. Certainly you can interview people who have done what you're proposing, but to really understand the business means having the courage to "live" the business for a period of time. If you have decided to open a restaurant, would you be willing to work part-time evenings or weekends as a dishwasher or busboy?

Entrepreneurial Start-Up (with and without partners)

Although you may be tempted to open up your business by yourself, going into a partnership has some advantages. Start-up financing may be easier. You can share the management load (hopefully). There is always someone who will have the same loyalty and drive as you (hopefully). You will each bring complementary skills (hopefully). And so on.

Make absolutely sure that you have a written partnership agreement.

The risks in partnership have to do with the word "hopefully." Nobody enters into a marriage with the expectation of divorce. But unless responsibilities and expectations are fully agreed to, and then "lived" on a daily basis by all partners, it is likely that the partnership will fall apart. And when that happens, the value of the business usually drops precipitously.

If you are going into a partnership, make absolutely sure that you have a written partnership agreement that includes, at least, a separation/dissolution/buy-out clause.[6] What else should be in the agreement? Division of responsibilities, determination of compensation, ownership structure, along with the answers to many "what-ifs." If you invest in nothing else, you and your partner(s) should spend money getting an appropriate legal agreement drafted.

Consultancy/Free Agent

If you have ever signed a contract with an IT services company or one of the major consulting outfits, you understand intimately their pricing: somewhere between $100 and $300 or even more per hour. For that fee, you get a number of things: the "guarantee" behind their name, a proven methodology, no training expenses, no HR administration

6. One form of this is the so-called shotgun clause. If partner A wishes to buy out partner B at a specific price, B can turn around and require A to sell the business to B at that specific price.

costs, and sundry other benefits. You supposedly also get top-notch staff who know their subject intimately, and can thus add value well beyond their cost.

Unfortunately, many of the "name shops" will use their senior people to sell the job, and the (albeit bright) juniors to actually execute. You will likely be stuck with a junior project manager, as only "Jim" was available for your timeframe. The project executive/program manager (who is supposed to "coach" the project manager) will instead be used to rescue the project as it starts to slide off the rails.

Hiring a consultant is very different from being one.

Becoming a free agent takes this model and turns it around. Your clients will get a top-flight consultant – you – who has the experience to solve their very pressing problems. Compared to these industry-outsider consultants who come up with recommendations and then leave, you have "felt the pain" and have the experience to solve problems realistically and pragmatically. Likely, your clients will expect to pay much less for your services than for the name-brand firms; this shouldn't be a problem for you, both because your overheads are far lower, and your net after-tax earnings will likely be higher due to your ability to write off a number of previously non-deductible expenses (such as home office).

Hiring a consultant, which you may have done before, is very different from being one. It can be hard to understand some of the stresses that come with this type of work. Your time must be split between selling and delivering your services, which are two very different types of skills. Whenever you are not working (for example, when you are on vacation, when you are selling, or when you are in training) you do not get paid. And you must realize that your big, corporately grown ego must be shunted aside, as consultants get all the blame when things go wrong, and none of the credit when things are successful. Another major change will be that of handling the billings and receivables. You learn to appreciate the "magic" of having your pay deposited automatically each month only when this no longer happens!

Many years ago, I did significant work for a client during the first 15 days of the month, and then, per our agreement, billed at the end of the month. They received the invoice at the beginning of the next month, put it in a 30-day "hold queue," and then paid it on the next payment cycle – the end of that month. I received my payment a week later. Effectively, I was the Bank of Randall Craig for three months! Worse, I had incurred out-of-pocket expenses on their behalf, so my business was not only financing time, but their expenses! For a quarter of the year! As a free agent, one learns very quickly about the difference between "It's in the mail" and having the money in your hand!

However, if you are the type of person who continually enjoys diving into the deep end, gets immense satisfaction from saying "I did that" (even if nobody else knows), and enjoys working with strong management teams across different organizations, then consulting is worth a try.

To test-drive consulting is not so easy, because the sell-cycle for any specific engagement is either too long, there is a time conflict with your current position (can't be in two places at once), or there is a business conflict with your current employer. To understand the business of consulting, consider talking to the independent consultants that you know, and read a few books on the subject. Two great books on the subject are *Managing the Professional Services Firm* and *The Trusted Advisor*, both by David Maister.

Another option, if consulting interests you, is to get a job at one of the large international consultancies. While each has its own criteria for hiring, usually mid-tier hires must have a unique quality, or they would not be hired:

- Strong enough business development skills to achieve a high margin beyond your salary.
- Special knowledge that can be exploited firm-wide. (e.g., if you helped draft specific legislation, or if you have an obscure technical skill.)

- Unique relationships that can be exploited firm-wide. (Usually these are exploited either for business development or lobbying purposes.)

If you do get hired under these circumstances, remember that your value to the consultancy generally ends when your unique quality is no longer unique. Unless you can parlay your job into something else relatively quickly, when your value ends, expect your job to end too.

Purchase an Existing Business

The major benefit of purchasing a business is that everything doesn't have to be started from scratch. Processes exist, people exist, systems exist; relationships with customers, suppliers, and the bank are usually long-standing, if not strong.

If you are purchasing a smaller enterprise, the biggest risk is that the customers will leave when the owner/manager does.

If you are purchasing a smaller enterprise, the biggest risk is that the customers will leave when the owner/manager does. The second biggest risk is that you are not able to successfully do the knowledge transfer from the outgoing owner/manager. If you are purchasing a medium or larger enterprise, the biggest risks usually revolve around the unfound skeletons in the closet and the quality of the management team. Even if you consider yourself an expert in the area, if you are looking to purchase a business, get professional help both for the negotiations and the due diligence. Thoughtfully consider what you learn from the due diligence prior to moving forward with any transaction.

It would be impossible to do justice to this alternative in a few pages; indeed, entire books have been written on the subject. Instead, we'll review four different purchase strategies: franchises, successions, structural change, and avocation.

Franchise Purchase

The benefit of running a franchise is that most of the thinking is already done for you. For your franchise fee (and many, many obligations under the franchise agreement), you slot yourself in, follow the manual, and operate. Usually, the franchise owner is on the front line themselves, often as much to reduce costs as to provide the management function.

For many readers of this book, franchise ownership may not be a fit. Of course, for some, "following the manual" is appealing, and for them, a particular franchise might be just the right thing. If you are interested, visit the franchise trade shows in your area.

A more proactive variation on this theme would be the purchase of a master franchise for your country or region. Essentially, you would license the name, operating manuals, and processes of a successful foreign franchise organization, make appropriate changes for your market, and become the franchisor within your territory. Master franchise agreements are a mechanism for the foreign franchisor to both earn "today income" and open new geographic regions, without committing capital or consuming management time.

To find a suitable master franchise candidate, consider spending time at foreign franchise trade shows. Less productive, but perhaps more fun, is to look for concepts as you do your personal travel abroad.

Succession Purchase

Especially in family-run businesses, succession planning is either neglected or not done as rigorously as it should be. By the time the majority owner is ready for retirement, internal (or family) leadership candidates are often long gone or uninterested. When there is no heir apparent, and the uninvolved family ownership group is looking to cash out, you may find an opportunity for an unsolicited offer.

If you do purchase this type of company, be prepared to deal with nepotism, as well as the effects of low infrastructure or technology investment.

Structural Change Purchase

An industry structure may change for a variety of reasons: changing technology, new channel entrants, mergers and acquisitions, vertical integration, changes in regulatory or political environments, just to name a few. If you believe that a particular industry (such as your current one) will not look the same in the future as it does now, you should consider purchasing a company that can be positioned to take advantage of that change.

Needless to say, the risks here are that your analysis is off, and the industry structure does change, but not exactly as you imagined it to. Mitigate your risk by testing out different change scenarios during the acquisition process, and then plan for those contingencies.

Mitigate your risk by testing out different change scenarios during the acquisition process.

Avocation Purchase

Business success is determined by both inspiration and perspiration. Perspiration is easy – most successful managers do this quite well, but where does the inspiration come from? Purchasing a business in an area of great personal interest makes inspiration easy.

A risk, however, is that your personal subjectivity and ego get in the way of your business judgment of the merits of the opportunity.

A colleague in my martial arts club, a black-belt, was a long-time salesman for industrial parts in the telecommunications sector. He had been training in karate for many years in a large city, and after being transferred back to his home town, started to teach karate part-time to maintain his own training. A number of years later, he was still teaching karate, and enjoying it. His day job, on the other hand, was stressful and uncertain: he didn't enjoy it at all. As sometimes happens, fate intervenes; in his case, a retail martial arts supply store was put up for sale. He took it and hasn't looked back since.

Let's consider his risks: he had no experience in retail, let alone how to run his own business. He also didn't have a plan beforehand. He didn't take any small business management courses, nor did he have a chance to test-drive a retail working experience. But what he lacked in knowledge, he more than made up with inspiration and perspiration. When the opportunity presented itself, he grabbed it. Bluebird indeed!

Generally the way to find acquisition candidates (whether they be successions, structural change, or avocation purchases) is to work your network. Tell your lawyer, accountant, bank manager, and insurance agent your acquisition criteria; they are well positioned to know of any potential opportunities.

Trading Up: Working at Another Big Company

This is certainly the most traditional external next step. You are the CFO of a $25-million company and seek a position as the CFO of a $50-million company. You are a manager with a portfolio of 15 products, and you seek a position with a portfolio of 25 or more. Or perhaps you are a former secretary who has been promoted to management several years ago, but seem to have hit a glass ceiling because of corporate "memories" of your admin past.

The most important reason that trading up is such an attractive option is that you will likely stay in the same, or similar, industry. You can keep and leverage both your knowledge and your contact base. You love what you do, but are looking for greater challenge on a higher scale.

Trading Down: Working at a Smaller Company

Like moving to a larger company, moving to a smaller company is also a conventional alternative. Many years ago, I decided to sell my beautiful BMW 5-series car and replace it with a tiny (and not particularly attractive) Suzuki Swift. I loved driving the BMW, but I didn't really need it and was looking to spend the money on other priorities at the time. When you make this type of a change – whether a car, house, or job – you must be prepared for it. The Suzuki didn't accelerate like the BMW, nor did it have power leather seats. The Suzuki dealer service wasn't up to the standards of BMW either. But it sure was cheap to fill up the tank! If you move to a smaller organization, be prepared for a few surprises of your own (both positive and negative), and go with the flow; it's a lot less stressful.

Why move to a smaller organization in the first place? This type of move is usually made for one of three reasons: Maybe you are looking for an increased scope of responsibility, or maybe for a new management challenge, like a turnaround. Or maybe you've just had too much of the "rat race" and are looking for a less stressful environment.

Increased Scope

Again, consider a person who is at the top of their functional ladder, but has made their mark in an organization that does not "cross-promote" into general management. (For example, a CFO who works in a company that takes the president from the marketing or sales side of the business.). One way for this person to become a company head is to accept the role of president in a smaller organization, prove themselves, and then trade up. While this may seem like a one-step backwards for two-steps forward approach, it gives you several benefits:

- The ability to learn the job in another organization. Don't forget, you may have had senior experience with only one company so far; developing general management skills somewhere else will help you cultivate a more flexible management style. This will pay off in the long run.
- Because you have already been (in the above example) a CFO for a larger company, you bring greater credibility in this area than a leader without the experience. As this area will be less of a risk for you, your full attention can be focused on learning how to fill the new role.

Turnaround (or other management challenge)

Smaller companies often have challenges that their bigger competitors have already met. These challenges can be financial (avoiding bankruptcy, going public), managing growth, or perhaps solving a particular operational problem. The company has determined that the best course of action is to recruit externally. They are looking for a candidate who can say "Been there, done that," and then actually get it done.

Why would you want to consider this type of situation? Again, it may be for the personal challenge and managerial growth, but another reason may be more practical. As part of your compensation, your package will likely include an equity component, and your upside may be quite high.

Of course, the downside is that if you are not successful in your objectives, you have a black mark on your résumé that you will eventually have to justify. This shouldn't preclude you from looking at turn-around situations, if that is what excites you: the risk of a "black mark" exists no matter what you choose to do.

"Too Much"

You are interviewing the company as much as they are interviewing you.

The organization that you have grown up with has likely matured too, and with that growth have come changes. Some of the changes (increased scope, promotions, authority, etc.) may have been positive, but some may not be to your liking. For example, you may be spending too much time travelling away from your family. Or you may have to spend several evenings each week at business functions. Or maybe the internal politics are too distracting.

For whatever reason, moving to a smaller organization may help solve some of these problems, if you make your choice properly.

Here's a different perspective: as organizations grow, they need different types of managers; by moving to a smaller organization, you are pre-emptively aligning your skills (and comfort) with that new organization.

If you haven't been to a job interview for a few years, you should keep this fact in mind: you're interviewing the company as much as they're interviewing you. In the end, they are looking to "buy" your big company experience, as much as you're looking to sell it.

Move to Government, Regulator, Association, etc.

With so much experience in your industry, you may have generated a public profile within it. Taking your "brand equity" and moving to an organization that either speaks for your industry or regulates it, is an interesting way for you to leverage your knowledge – while providing you with a different intellectual spin.

You will have to feel comfortable with a number of changes if you make this type of move, most having to do with the differences between the for-profit and the not-for-profit dimension of the organization.

Attributes such as speed may rank far behind attributes such as equity, need, or public accountability.

NON-FINANCIAL OBJECTIVES ARE PRIMARY: You're likely used to a system that pressures for higher sales with lower costs. But are you prepared for organizational performance being ranked primarily by non-financial objectives? Would you remain personally motivated without a traditional financial scorecard?

STAKEHOLDER DIFFERENCES: In the corporate setting, the number one stakeholder groups are usually defined to be customers, then variously shareholders, employees, the community, and if applicable, regulators. We tend to value "focus," spend most of our time with one or two of these groups, and keep the rest on maintenance mode. In a not-for-profit, the weightings are skewed differently, often with the community, regulators, and special interest groups nearing the very top of the list and having real weight.

SENSE OF URGENCY: Most organizations understand the importance of speed, from the impact of a faster product development cycle on costs, to the impact that faster customer service has on customer retention. The Internet, and all the expectations it has engendered, has heightened pressure for speed even further. In many non-profits (and many areas of government), a sense of urgency just does not exist, as the incentive for speed is not as great as in the corporate world. And in some organizations, attributes such as speed rank far behind attributes such as equity, need, or public accountability.

PERSONNEL POLICIES: Staff retention and longevity are usually very high for non-profits, regulators, and associations, often because the jobs tend not to be pressured the way corporate jobs are. Unfortunately, in some non-profits, retention is high because there are often poor (or non-existent) personnel policies and practices. For organizations that use them, there is the additional complication of volunteers: it is hard to harness them, and as a result, hard to fire or discipline them.

Earn a Graduate Degree or Professional Certification (full- or part-time)

"Any port in a storm" is the strategy that is often used by the newly laid-off to justify the pursuit of an advanced education. While not very strategic, an educational pursuit is a rationale that can be easily explained to prospective employers when the job search begins yet again, in earnest.

For those looking to leave the Mother Ship without a "helping push" from uncooperative bosses (e.g., without a severance payment), deciding to pursue any type of full-time studies means a substantial financial sacrifice, often for two years or more. Despite these financial consequences, there may be some important reasons for doing so anyway:

- **GLASS CEILING ISSUE:** If you are a treasurer looking to become a CFO, you might find fewer opportunities unless you have either an MBA or accounting certification. You may be a teacher looking to move into curriculum design; yet without an M.Ed., you might never be considered for the position.
- **DESIRE FOR CAREER SHIFT:** After many years climbing through a functional silo, you understand many of the related jobs, but need a formal education for qualification. Examples include a bookkeeper who decides to become an accountant, an insurance underwriter who decides to become an actuary, a nurse who wishes to become a physical therapist, or a lay leader who wishes to become a cleric.
- **PERSONAL NEED FOR INTELLECTUAL CHALLENGE:** You may feel that you haven't been using your "head" much during

the last number of years, and that doing intensive study for several years will give you an intellectual jump-start. Review your Job Quality Checklist results. How did you answer the question about appropriate intellectual challenge?

- **ACADEMIC CAREER ENTRY POINT:** Pretty much the only way to become a college or university professor is to earn a PhD; unfortunately, these are almost impossible to do on a part-time basis.

You may be in a position where your employer provides matching donations to charities, including colleges and universities. If the normal annual tuition was $20,000, perhaps you could arrange to make a "donation" of $12,000 (in lieu of normal tuition), which was then matched dollar-for-dollar by your employer. The college does better by $4,000, as do you, by $8,000.

From a financial perspective, spend time reviewing the scholarships and grants that are available, both from public and private sources. Many large reference libraries, bookstores, and web sites have entire sections devoted to this subject. And some of the awards are significant.

It is worthwhile also exploring the options for pursuing advanced education on a part-time basis. While it may take longer to complete your studies, you will not suffer the financial consequences of zero income, nor have the immediate post-graduation uncertainty of finding another position. Your current employer may even cover some or all of your costs. This option can be appealing if it provides exactly what is missing from your current workplace: intellectual challenge.

"Job, Family, MBA: choose two."

The problem with part-time education, especially if it is a heavy load, is the cost it imposes on personal relationships. Indeed, an expression that is often repeated among new part-time MBA students is "Job, Family, MBA: choose two." If you try to "choose three," make sure the choice is one that is understood by all parties concerned: you, your spouse, and your workplace. Otherwise, you may learn of the other popular name for the MBA: the divorce course.

"Volunteer" and Community Service Work as a Full-Time Vocation

Very few people have the financial independence to quit paid work and donate their time 100% to the community, but if you can, why not consider it? Often, there is a dearth of strong leaders and managers in community service work, precisely because the best are often looking to establish the financial independence you already have.

If a full-time donation is impossible, spending some of your time doing volunteer work can still pay off. The return on your time investment certainly will be in personal satisfaction, but it can also be in strong relationships with other senior people in the community.

If you are nearing the end of your career, this may also be a way for you to test-drive a second career in the non-profit sector.

Reduce Work Week to 80%

What would happen if you worked each day only until 3:30 p.m.? Or worked only Monday to Thursday? How would you use your extra time? The list can grow quite a bit, but the alternatives are generally very appealing:

- Spend time with your children when they get home from school.
- Care for an elderly parent.
- Gardening and household improvements.
- Upgrade your education or training.
- Volunteer at your favorite charity.
- Golf, or some other hobby.
- Train for a marathon.
- Take piano or guitar lessons.
- Just relax.

Before you discard this alternative as one that is impossible financially, first determine how much the cut would actually cost. Most progressive employers won't cut your benefits, unless your "full-time" weekly hours go below a set floor – often 25 or 30 hours.

Determine how much the cut would actually cost.

If you reduce to an 80% schedule, it is your gross pay that is cut, not your net. After tax, depending on your tax bracket, your net pay might not take as much of a hit as you think. Furthermore, if you get a car as a benefit, you may be able to negotiate for a less expensive car (or at least the same model with fewer options), but more salary.

Here are some ideas to help you negotiate this type of arrangement:

- Ensure that you have a plan as to how the "other 20%" of your responsibilities will be handled. This will likely be the biggest issue you will have to address.
- Redefine job objectives and goals to account for your reduced schedule.
- Indicate your flexibility: if a meeting can be held only at a time when you are not in the office, you will make all efforts to attend.
- Find others in the organization who have successfully been able to negotiate a reduced work schedule; ask them about their experience both negotiating the arrangement and living it.
- Build in a meeting one month into the new arrangement to discuss how it is proceeding. If there are problems, it's best to formally address them while they're still small.

One of my clients relates an interesting story. Upon return from maternity leave several years ago, she found herself with a new manager. The old manager was a classic one-dimensional wonder, and my client was concerned that the new manager would be too. When my client was asked by her new manager what she was looking for in her job, she told him, and also mentioned in passing that a four-day work week would be desirable. Two weeks after meeting the manager, he called her into his office and told her it was set, if she was interested. Years later, she is still working a reduced work schedule successfully. While her manager was quite exceptional (and still is), this story illustrates well the adage "if you don't ask, you don't get!"

If you don't ask, you don't get!

The major risk in this kind of arrangement is one that increases as one rises in seniority. As a junior manager, work sharing, reduced schedules, and short-term leaves are relatively easy to manage, as others typically will fill in while you are not there. As an executive, though, your company pretty much buys "all" of you: nights, weekends, breakfast, lunch, and dinner. You are expected to run at 120% in order to meet your agreed-upon objectives. There are few who can fill in for you while you're not around. The more senior you get, the more likely you'll find yourself being paid 80% *for the same 120% effort*!

If you are able to address these issues, you will still need to monitor your colleagues' perceptions. Unless everyone understands your time boundaries, people may believe you to be slacking, and you will end up paying the political price for it.

Stay at Home with Kids or Parents

Your children are children only once. And once your parents have passed away, they are gone forever. Unfortunately, we realize only too late how little time we actually spend with both of these groups. Deciding to spend time with your loved ones precisely when they need it gives personal satisfaction well beyond any money that the next step in your career can provide.

Many people today feel that this option is closed, mainly for financial reasons. While this concern is true for some, if you have the will, you can find a way.

Others may look at this option and be concerned about what others will say. If this happens, think about what your children or parents would say. Don't want to be labelled a "househusband" or "housewife"? Just remember the reason you're doing it. The negative comments given by others are more a reflection on them than on you.

If you decide to be a full-time caregiver, you will likely miss the stimulation and challenge of the working world. Consider taking on the occasional consulting assignment to keep sharp, and increasing your community involvement to take up the slack.

While plans often change, decide on a timeframe after which you will return to the workforce – whether it be three months, two years, or until a particular milestone. This will help structure your time (particularly with community involvement), and give you a better "story" to tell upon your return.

Do Something Non-traditional

There is really no limit to the possibilities of how you can spend your time. In fact, the concept of "non-traditional" itself is a relative term. My wife's family has been in the medical profession (doctors, dentists, nurses, optometrists, etc.) for generations. When she went into business taking a corporate position, she was considered very non-traditional: quite scandalous, actually! Many sons and daughters of family businesses are also considered non-traditional when they too decide to pursue something outside the family.

So what does "non-traditional" really mean? Perhaps all it means is a job choice that would surprise others in your peer and family group; perhaps all it means is a job choice that you haven't yet considered.

If your career has been in the corporate world, for example, some decidedly non-corporate job choices might be to become a writer, work in a developing country, go into politics, or become an interior designer.

Once you make your decision, you can expect a broad range of reactions from those around you:

- "You're crazy!"
- "Lots of courage – good for you!"
- "Why would you want to do that?"
- "That's what I would do, if I only could!"

- "How can you make that kind of decision?"
- "Let's see how long that lasts…"

Some of these reactions are borne of misunderstanding; people assuming that you are driven by the same forces that drive them. As a result, they don't understand how your decision could possibly make sense. Other reactions are from people close to you, where there is a concern about how a change will affect them. And others will have a genuine concern about whether or not you are making the right decision. In all these cases, helping them understand how and why you came to your decisions will help reduce their stress, and yours.

For those people who are not close to you, do not feel that you need to explain anything if you don't want to; your decision is none of their business. On the other hand, dealing with nosy people can help you come to terms with your decision, by forcing you to confront head-on, and defend, your choice.

KEY POINTS

There are many, many options that are available. Some will hold more personal interest than others. As you go through the list, ask yourself "Why not" to each of them.

Chapter 10: Making the Choice to Go

Let's close the argument for good about staying versus going. Fact: everyone will leave the Mother Ship; the only questions are when, and by whose choice.

It's safe to say that most would prefer to leave of their own volition. If you have not reconciled the *when* question exactly for yourself, let's assume that it is within the year. This assumption removes the last obstacle to making the choice: there is no reason *not* to start your planning.

In the very worst case (which is that you get fired unexpectedly), any planning you will have completed is work that can be re-used for job-search purposes. If the one-year assumption is wrong and you haven't left by the end of the year, once again, much of your planning will already be done for when you *are* ready to leave.

So, how to decide where to go?

One of my early managers, a financial wizard, gave me some advice: "You can only swim upstream for so long, before packing it in." One of my later managers, a marketing wiz, also gave me some advice: "Winners always differentiate themselves, like the fish that swims upstream. Better to be the fish than a lemming." There are truths in both these statements. The head of HR at a large multinational probably said it worst: "Better a bad day of fishing than a good day at work." From the head of HR? Sheesh!

Happiness, recognition, power, financial security – these are some of the end-points that your day job can provide. But what is it that has given you your success to date: your drive, education, experience, acumen, or just plain luck? Whatever it happens to be, your personal strengths (and a bit of luck) will be what continues to drive your success. The challenge, of course, is making the right choice and then converting idea into action.

Earlier in the book, you went through a number of diagnostic exercises to help determine when to go (SkillChecks, Job Quality Checklist), and exercises that expose context

(Personal Balance Sheet, Reality Check Interviews). We will now use the results of these exercises for a different purpose: helping make the choice about *where* to go next.

Right from the start, you can probably cross a few of the options off the list. For example, you may already have a graduate degree, or you may have no desire to be a homemaker. But – let's not get too quick about crossing off so many at once. At the risk of too much repetition, now is the time to go through an exercise of asking "Why not?" for each path. What would it take for you to actually choose a particular path? If you are near the very beginning of your thinking, consider the following exercise: **For each option, write one paragraph describing the changes in your life that would be needed in order to be successful with that option.**

Another question concerns the criteria, other than "gut," that we should use to make the right choice. Thankfully, you have completed most of the heavy lifting earlier. We'll use the SkillChecks, Job Quality Checklist, Personal Balance Sheet, and the Reality Check interview notes to filter the options. (Hint: if you haven't completed these diagnostic exercises in earnest, now would be a good time to do so!)

Rank each option based on the SkillChecks, Job Quality Checklist, Personal Balance Sheet, and the Reality Check interview notes.

Throughout this process, you will rank each of the options, so that at the end of the analysis, your preferences will be clear.

Review SkillChecks

Recall, when you initially did the SkillChecks, it was in the context of where you are at the present time. Let's now use the same information, but in the context of what will come next. For example, from SkillCheck I:

- Have you veered away from the area of your initial training and are interested in "returning to your roots"? Do any of the options suggest that this may be possible?
- Was there something from earlier in your career (or education) that interested you, but you never followed up on, and that is related to a current opportunity?

- Which options take advantage of your "excellent" skills?
- Which options have most in common with the most fun parts of your previous positions?
- Which options incorporate your non-work interests?
- Which options should have a lower priority because you are not strong in those areas?

Each SkillCheck I question can generate many different career possibilities. As you review, consider the following SkillCheck I question more closely: "What non-work activities provide you the most satisfaction? What is it about these activities that interest you?" Your answer can provide valuable clues if you are looking to change career directions. Perhaps you enjoy traveling or working with children. Maybe you like working with your hands, or being outdoors.

What non-work activities provide you the most satisfaction?

If you like being on stage, for example, that might indicate several interesting career possibilities: instructing aerobics, teaching school, going into television journalism, or acting. While doing any of these directly might be hard to picture, there are *indirect* career options that relate to this list that might be more realistic: opening an aerobics studio, being the CFO of a private school, becoming the VP of sales at a media outlet, or providing financial planning for actors.

For each of the SkillCheck I questions, pull together a list of potential career possibilities, along with any indirect career options that relate to them.

SkillCheck II also suggests some criteria:

- Which options relate directly to areas where you are considered a "guru"?
- Which options might have lower priority because they rely on skills where you only have gaps?

After answering these questions for both SkillChecks, and completing a list of potential career possibilities, review the options again. Have one or two been eliminated? Have one or two moved up the priority list?

Review Job Quality Checklist

When you first did the Job Quality Checklist, you did it for your existing job. At this point, the Job Quality Checklist can be used to contrast each remaining option.

For example, if the idea of being an entrepreneur and starting your own business appeals to you, how might the actual "job" rate against these criteria? Effectively, each dimension (Fun, Challenge, Like your colleagues, Goals, Balance, and Compensation) is an additional criteria that you can use. The table, shown below, is a generic, high-level example of the analysis you should do for each alternative:

- Entrepreneurial Start-up.
- Entrepreneur with Partners.
- Consultancy/Free Agent.
- Consultant Within a Large Firm.
- Franchise Purchase.
- Succession Purchase.
- Structural Change Purchase.
- Avocation Purchase.
- Trading Up: Working at Another Big Company.
- Trading Down: Working at a Smaller Company.
- Move to Government, Regulator, Association, etc.
- Earn a Graduate Degree or Professional Certification (full or part-time).
- Volunteer and Community Service Work.
- Reduced Work Week.
- Stay at Home with Kids or Parents.
- Do Something Non-traditional.

Job Quality Checklist: Entrepreneur

FUN: At the macro level, since you're doing something of your own choice, of course it is fun! Peel back the layers, however, and there will likely be some major ups and downs. For example, as the president, it's fun. As the janitor and mailroom clerk, maybe not so much so. From my own experience, though, doing the unpleasant tasks for your own business are not as onerous as doing them for someone else's.

CHALLENGE: You'll be doing many tasks for the first time; you'll also be playing new organizational roles for the first time. No problem with challenge here.

LIKE YOUR COLLEAGUES: Since you are choosing them yourself, this is likely not a problem. And if you really, really don't like them, you can always let them go. Ironically, the problem with being an entrepreneur may be that you may not have enough colleagues, at least in the very beginning stages.

GOALS: You would need to answer this one in your own context. Presumably, some of the options move you closer to your goals than others.

BALANCE: Starting a business and looking for balance? In practically all cases, there is *no* balance as an entrepreneur. Of course, you might be different, but expect to give up considerably on everything except the business. After the business stabilizes, though, your time is yours to use as you wish.

COMPENSATION: At the beginning, don't look for a big payday. Being an entrepreneur is all about the chase: building something that has enduring value, and then capturing that value when it has matured. If you are the type of person who is worried about certainty of personal income, and who won't be able to sleep at night because of fears of not making payroll, then this dimension isn't looking good for you.

When you go through this exercise yourself, it should be far more specific and more "me-centric." Think about how different this analysis might be for a retail store compared to an advertising agency or a financial consultancy. Also, the more refined your business idea is, the more relevant your analysis will be.

After completing this review (Fun, Challenge, Like your colleagues, Goals, Balance, and Compensation) for each of the options, some may fall off the list, while others suddenly look more interesting. Spend some time to rank each in terms of your relative interest.

Review Your Personal Balance Sheet

How does each option move you toward your next goal, along each Personal Balance Sheet dimension of Community, Family, Intellectual, Spiritual, Physical, Financial, and Career? Some options will move you faster, others more slowly.

The issue isn't just how quickly you might realize a goal; the issue is also *how your balance will change* from the status quo.

The issue isn't just how quickly you might realize a goal; the issue is also *how your balance will change* from the status quo if you go down any particular path. Questions that follow include whether the balance realignment is acceptable to both you and your family. Is there a time element to any of the options – would the balance shift over time? Using the entrepreneur example from above, the first year or two are "make or break" times, and you will have to pay the price with very little balance. Several years later, you may have others doing most of the work and your balance will be different yet again.

Look at the final column of your Personal Balance Sheet, where you wrote down your criteria for success. Consider these criteria yet again: for each option you might choose, which Personal Balance Sheet dimension will be satisfied, and which will not?

You may be considering eliminating some options just because you're not willing to pay the price. Rather than discarding options so quickly, consider how you can mitigate the "price" of each potential discard. Perhaps, using the entrepreneur example again, doing it with a partner might help. Or perhaps you should explore financing alternatives: do you look for external funding first, or try to grow the business on a shoestring before approaching lenders?

When you have completed this analysis, revise your rankings of each alternative if you need to do so.

Review Reality Check Interview Notes

Likely, the results of the interviews have already figured prominently in your planning and ranking activities. But now is the time to review your rough interview notes again.

COMMON THREADS: These are the common comments made by many of your interviewees that struck a chord in you. Perhaps they all identified your strengths. Perhaps they all saw you operating in a particular role, or position, or industry vertical. Are any of these in common with the options you are considering? If yes, great. If no, ask yourself why; if you feel comfortable with the answer anyway, then don't worry about it.

DISSENTING OPINIONS: While most of your interviewees saw you one way, perhaps one or two people saw something that others didn't. Maybe they were in the best (or only) position to notice a particular skill or unique ability. Does this ability point more to one or another of the options? Again, do not close doors too early; honestly consider whether there is validity in the dissenting observation.

After considering the common threads and dissenting opinions, re-rank each of the options. Hopefully, at this point, one or two of them are looking more like favorites.

Making the Final Choice

In the unlikely event that you have it exactly figured out, congratulations! Otherwise, read on:

In the end, it will be your passion that fuels your success.

What if you still have no idea which option best fits? Did you go through each of the diagnostic exercises (SkillChecks, Job Quality Checklist, Personal Balance Sheet, Reality Check), entirely and honestly? The thinking time that these require is what generates their value. Consider redoing one or more of these, at a greater depth, especially if you just "scanned" the exercises earlier.

However, could it be that you're just a bit afraid of making a commitment to any one of the options? Surely this is unlikely, but it's true that leaving the Mother Ship is very difficult to do. If you feel apprehensive, force yourself to make a choice anyway. As you fill in the gaps (Chapter 11), you will begin to develop more confidence in your choice, and with this confidence, you'll also develop the courage to commit. (And if you become even less certain of your choice, consider yourself fortunate: it isn't too late to change your plan!)

What if it is hard to choose between two alternatives? Assuming they are ranked very closely on all the scales above, your analysis has to go one step further. First assess the different risk and return levels between the two front-runners. Then consider how different the preparation and gap-filling for each alternative would be. All other things being equal, if one alternative requires significantly less preparation, then choose it! Once you have added these new variables (risk/return and preparation effort) to the mix, one of the options should move slightly ahead.

All of your analysis cannot describe why certain opportunities are more appealing than others. In the end, it will be your passion that fuels your success. So in the end, despite all the exercises and logic, go with the option that has captured your heart as well as your mind.

What if you have decided on an option (say, to be an entrepreneur), but you don't know what *type* of business to start? Go back to your SkillChecks, and look at where you are rated a guru. Review your Reality Check Interview notes, and look at the common threads. Did your interviewees suggest (or even hint) at something? And finally, consider asking your friends and family for their suggestions, again. You never know what might come up.

Only when you quit – when the trigger is pulled – is your choice actually locked down. Your "choice" up to this point is important *only for the purposes of your planning.* And as you fill in the gaps, plans can, and will, change.

KEY POINTS

- All the direction-setting exercises you have completed (SkillChecks, Job Quality Checklist, Personal Balance Sheet, and Reality Check Interviews) can now be re-used as personalized criteria for making your choice.
- Using them this way, you may find you need to go back and revise some of your earlier work. This is to be expected: as your direction becomes more focused, your analysis demands greater precision as well.

ACTION CHECKLIST

❑ Job Quality Checklist

Chapter 11: Filling in the Gaps

There is a time of special opportunity that exists between your decision to go and when you actually leave. You have separated yourself psychologically from the Mother Ship. You have decided, at least preliminarily, what you will do next. And you still have a regular income. Until the trigger is pulled, you must spend your time on activities that can best prepare you for when you do leave. Everyone recognizes the maxim of "no risk, no return." But that doesn't mean you should take risks that can be mitigated by properly using your time appropriately beforehand.

While it may seem strange, many of these risk-mitigating and preparatory activities have more to do with *you* than with what you will be doing when you leave. There are several reasons for this:

- You've spent most of your career in one place, and you've taken on many of the characteristics and habits of that organization. Some of these, such as *procrastination, busywork,* and your *self-image,* may need examination.
- Before you go, you may be able to try out new things, without worrying too much about making a big mistake and poisoning the well.
- Whether you're moving to another organization or starting one of your own, people are buying *you.* Especially at the beginning, you may not have the internal network of skills and support that you are used to; anything you can do to improve yourself before you arrive will pay dividends handsomely.

Some activities will help you prepare for later (Networking, Avoiding Planning Paralysis), while others relate more to logistics and administration.

You Can Control Only What You Can Control

As a teenager, I had a summer job in a hardware store. Since I had to take two buses to get there, timing was always a bit of a gamble. This was a problem because the manager got terribly upset (e.g., "You're fired") if staff members weren't punctual. One day, when I was waiting for the first bus, feeling stressed about the time, it struck me. No matter how much I worried, and how many times I paced back and forth, the bus wasn't going to reach the stop any earlier. And when the bus did come, I certainly wouldn't be able to make it go any faster. So I got out my book and was able to read a few chapters en route. When I had that epiphany, I also realized that the worry (and stress) of being late wasn't caused by a threatening manager, but rather by me internally.

As you're filling in the gaps, don't worry about what isn't really necessary – and don't worry about what you can't control. Think instead about what is within your power to change. While I couldn't control the speed of the bus once I was on it, I sure could have caught an earlier one.

What is "really necessary" and what is not? Tasks, priorities, people, and processes that help you focus are necessary; anything that distracts you from your goal likely is not.

Think of how your company (or department) has maintained its focus over the years. Conventional wisdom and the business press have spawned dozens of useful sayings: define core competencies, stick to your knitting, customer care, etc. Has your organization adopted any of these? Likely, quite a few. Think of your corporate funding decisions, for example. When there is plenty of cash, new projects tend to be funded; when cash is tight, the oxygen of cash goes only to the most important, core parts of the organization.

Start with the most important "core" activities on your list.

As you fill in the gaps, you must start with the most important "core" activities on your list. Then, with diminishing marginal benefit, the less important activities can come later. If a triggering event happens, you have to be ready to run – hopefully with as many of the important gaps filled as possible.

While this is easily said, two obstacles can prevent this from happening: procrastination and busywork, and one that kills your personal excellence: the problem with getting a "B."

Procrastination

It is ironic that we spend more time on business-related planning than on our personal planning. Why is that? Do we find it is easier to do one than the other because we've been shown how to do *business*, but no one has shown us how to do *personal*? Or is it because we are procrastinating? Probably a bit of both. *Leaving the Mother Ship* applies process to career planning, so it can help with the *personal*. Procrastination can be addressed only by first recognizing it, then developing the discipline to avoid it.

Every minute that we delay is a minute away from the important things that we must make time for: think of your Personal Balance Sheet. These goals are things we *need* to do, not optional activities that we may *want* to do. When we procrastinate, we substitute required *needs* for desired *wants*: we kill progress!

We sometimes pretend that a task doesn't exist merely because we don't want to see it, like an ostrich with its head firmly in the sand. Once we pluck our head out and look around, what was once a small problem often has grown considerably. When we put off something that is a higher priority, we needlessly add stress to our lives.

When we put off something that is a higher priority, we needlessly add stress to our lives.

Every minute that we delay also adds risk. If a triggering event happens, and we haven't filled enough of the important gaps, we are more likely than not to make poor decisions after we leave.

Busywork

Have you ever quickly grabbed a chocolate bar and a soft drink for lunch? Busywork is to your time like empty calories are to nutrition. The chocolate bar and soft drink may be tremendously satisfying while you're eating them, but they displace important vitamins and other nutrients that your body needs. Busywork takes up your available time, displacing important priorities that really should be seen to first. In a sense, busywork is a form of procrastination.

Think of the scenario where you have ten things on your task list. One is a critical presentation to a prospect, due two days from now. The other nine items are things that are relatively unimportant, due next week. With effort, you can deal with all nine of them within a few hours. Do you focus exclusively on the presentation, or do you get rid of the nine unimportant items first? Intellectually, most people will say that the presentation is the priority. When it comes to practice, though, there are no shortages of rationales for doing the exact opposite:

- **"Killing the nine little things means I can concentrate on the priority."** This is the "reduce my stress" argument. Think about it: if there is time to do both before the presentation is due, why not do the presentation first – just in case?
- **"If I deal with the nine little things first, then I won't hold up the nine folks who need my input."** This is the "I'm indispensable" argument. Surely having them wait two days isn't going to make a difference? And if one of these nine items becomes critical along the way, you can change your decision as to which item gets your immediate attention at that time.
- **"I've always hated doing presentations; I'll be more comfortable if I do the other stuff first."** This is the "fear and uncertainty" argument. If we are afraid of doing something, because of either a bad experience or inexperience, we think that doing it last will magically increase our confidence level. Logic suggests the opposite: the less comfort we have with a task, the more time we need to do it, and thus the earlier we should start it.

People who do the busywork first tend to use large amounts of personal time to fit in their priorities. Some, having finished their work late at night, have a great feeling of satisfaction for having so much "output." Others are just plain tired.

So how do you avoid the evils of procrastination and busywork? Each person is different. Nevertheless, here are some basic ideas you might try:

- Recognize when you are procrastinating or doing busywork. (Then stop doing it!)
- Schedule (and budget) your time, then keep to that schedule.
- Set up your to-do list the night before.
- Take a course on time management.

You can control only what you can control. If there is a magic bullet against procrastination and busywork, as one of my former managers repeated over and over, it is **Focus – Focus – Focus.**

The Problem with Getting a "B"

If you ask your children, or worse, your children's teachers, whether 70% is an acceptable mark, the answer will likely be "Absolutely: a 'B' is great," followed by the comment that while an "A" would be better, not everyone can get an "A." This attitude, which is where mediocrity gets its beginnings, poisons us both in school and at work. When we evaluate our staff, how many of them are happy with a rating of "above average" and no longer strive for a "superstar" rating? From a management perspective, if they are satisfied with a 70%, is there not a conflict with a "100% customer satisfaction" philosophy?

No one wants a kick in the pants, but an evaluation of (say) 55% often will spur real change. An effort of greater than 90% usually means a high resolve already exists. A score of 70%, unfortunately, will not spur change and is not an indicator of an excellent resolve: hence the problem with getting a "B." If you are right 70% of the time, by definition you are wrong three times out of ten. Would you be satisfied with a surgeon or a pilot doing their jobs wrong 30% of the time?

Would you be satisfied with a surgeon or a pilot doing their jobs wrong 30% of the time?

The relevance to us as managers and leaders (and especially to a person who is considering leaving the Mother Ship) is that merely recognizing that 70% is not acceptable will often mark you as different. And the difference between a 70%

organization and a 100% organization is the difference between success and failure in what you do next in your career.

While you are both doing your day job *and* filling in the gaps, there is really no room for anything less than 100% personal effort and excellence. Otherwise, you will be either compromising your current position or reducing your chance of success after you leave.

Opening Closed Doors

One of the ugly things we do, often without realizing it, is label things. Why? It helps us to categorize an item, and later to remember it. Unfortunately, a funny thing often happens – the item begins to take on the characteristics of the label itself. This is relevant in our context for two reasons: we often label other people, and we unwittingly label ourselves.

Labels needlessly limit our potential.

Think about the last time you tried a new sport. Did you think, "I am uncoordinated, so this will be tough," or did you think, "I am a natural athlete, so I expect to be good at this"? In either case, your self-label ("uncoordinated" or "athletic") will have an impact on your mindset, and this mindset will have a real-life impact on your success in that sport. Giving unhelpful labels is something we also do to those closest to us, and unfortunately, our friends and family often will live up to the label: "not good at reading," "can't control their weight," "bad car driver," "doesn't dress appropriately," etc.

It is always satisfying to see someone spring open an artificially closed door. My father, a retired senior executive, had always "recognized" that he was physically not flexible. When it came to sports, he avoided activities that required flexibility and took up ones that emphasized other athletic attributes, such as focus, endurance, and speed. Only after trying Pilates did he realize that he could have developed significant flexibility, if only he had started stretching long ago.

We often live our business lives within the boundaries of the labels we give ourselves too. Are we "no good at numbers," "not the best salesperson," or "technically inept"? It is worthwhile examining carefully, and perhaps modifying, our own self-labels, as they can help us focus our next business or activity. Once we take the leap, an improved self-identity will reduce the risk of failure.

Exercise in Self-Labelling

1. Using a chart similar to the one below, write down all the labels that you think apply to yourself, separating the positive and negative ones.
2. For each of them, write down the first event (or events) that convinced you the label is accurate.
3. Then, write down a different event that actually refuted the negative label.
4. For those negative labels where there is no refuted event, put together a plan to succeed: a plan, which once completed, will prove to you that the negative label no longer holds true. Executing this plan is what opens a closed door.

Negative Labels (examples)

Label	First event	Refuted event (or plan)
Unathletic	Always last one picked for team as a kid; dropped Phys Ed as soon as possible	Earned Black Belt as an adult
Insensitive to staff	As first-time manager, staff wanted to transfer	Earned loyalty of subordinates in next management job
Can't do presentations	Messed up presentation when at university, and have avoided presentations since	PLAN: take a public speaking course, videotape presentation rehearsals, present to smaller audiences more frequently to develop comfort
(etc.)		
(etc.)		

Positive Labels (examples)

Label	First event
Great at sales	Sold lottery tickets at high school
Group organizer	Put together band during university
Driven	Client comments about me as project manager on first large assignment
(etc.)	
(etc.)	

An interesting demonstration of the power of labels occurred several years ago at a sales conference my company held. The final session included a motivational speaker to fire up the troops. There were 25 of us, sitting around a large, U-shaped conference table. The speaker picked one of the larger, stronger individuals as a volunteer. While the speaker held the volunteer's arms to his side, she asked him to lift his arms above his head. He was able to do so easily, breaking her grip.

Then she told him that she was going to berate him for five minutes, and that he would try lifting his hands again. She called him a slew of ugly names: incompetent, uncoordinated, and fat were just a few, and she elaborated on each of them for his and the audience's benefit. He was then asked to lift his arms above his head. To the surprise of everyone there, he could not do it! No one was more surprised than the volunteer himself.

She repeated the experiment again, but this time with complimentary labels: smart, strong, creative, athletic, etc. She also asked the audience to give him a rousing round of applause. He then lifted his arms effortlessly, despite the speaker's tight grip.

I asked him later what had happened. He said he certainly wasn't faking it. He just did not know. What really happened in this case was that when the labels were applied, he believed them subconsciously; he then conformed to those labels. He artificially closed doors for himself.

Look back at your self-labeling exercise (you did do the exercise, didn't you?). Consider how your career has progressed over the years as you have abided by these labels. Had you missed early promotions because you "weren't a numbers person"? What if you could rely on the strength of your presentations – instead of avoiding them because you were "always bad at presentations"?

As you consider the career options described earlier, remember that the label you give yourself is *your* label that *you* give *yourself!* Leaving negative labels behind is just as important as remembering the positive ones you take with you. **Action: Fill in the gaps by following your plan to remove negative labels. Open those doors!**

Labelling hurts those outside of work as well. If you have children, have you labelled them too? "Jennifer is a real beauty, while Sam is the thinker in the family."

What if Jennifer develops to be a slightly heavier teenager, but brilliant academically? She might become so preoccupied with her appearance, that she neglects her true gift of scholarship. Or Sam, who might really like sports, but never tries out for the football team, because he has to study so hard to maintain his imposed image of being "the thinker".

Just like the labels we give ourselves, the labels we give those closest to us stick – and can artificially close even the most promising of doors.

Your Personal Balance Sheet – in Action

In Chapter 8, you defined a number of goals along each of the Personal Balance Sheet dimensions: Community, Family, Intellectual, Spiritual, Physical, Financial, and Career. For each of these, you had also defined the criteria for success. While you are filling in the gaps, much of your attention should be focused on the Career dimension. But what about the others?

Most people, when they complete the Personal Balance Sheet, see an embarrassing gap between their goals and accomplishments. Since there are only so many hours in each day, having an extreme focus on one dimension (e.g., career) by definition means that there must be less emphasis on others. As your decision to leave was made in the context of your Personal Balance Sheet, it only makes sense to look at your Personal Balance Sheet once again. Filling in the gaps is not only about getting ready to leave; it is about making sure that when you leave, you achieve all your goals.

Add a final extra column onto the chart: action plan. For each dimension on the Personal Balance Sheet, review your goals and write down the steps to achieving them. For example, if your Community goal was for greater involvement, and you wanted to achieve this by organizing an annual neighborhood fun day, your action plan would define each of the steps necessary to make the fun day happen.

Especially if your day job does not bring the fulfillment you require, investing time in other goal-oriented activities is energizing. Once you have reasonable plans against each dimension, devote time to actually making them happen. Writing a plan doesn't achieve results – executing it does.

Networking

How many people do you know? What is the strength of those relationships? Consider your college graduating class – how many could you call on the telephone and have a decent conversation with, let alone have them remember your name without prompting?

If you are like most people, you remember those who have meaning to you (both personal and professional). Those whom you have little time for – well, you have little time for them, and the relationship lapses.

Your network is a long-term asset that grows more valuable over time. Before you leave the Mother Ship, your network can provide insight into different business options, it can help with the Reality Check process, and it can set an example for you about life away from the Mother Ship. After you leave, the network is even more precious. It can provide business leads, introductions to target clients, valuable business advice, and much-needed personal support.

How do you measure the strength of your personal network? Consider the following exercise, taken from the insurance industry but very applicable here. New recruits are asked to identify their natural market – that is, those whom they have a relationship with. The exercise is simple. Write down 150 people whom you have a relationship with, and then rank how each person sees *their relationship with you* – either good, neutral, bad, or lapsed. Consider categorizing this list, perhaps by how you met each person (college, former supplier, family relation, etc.) If you can write down 150 names easily, keep adding 25 people until you honestly cannot write down any more. If you are having trouble coming up with 150 names, write down as many as you can, then push yourself to find another 25.

Were you surprised by how many (or how few) people were on your list? Were you a bit embarrassed about how many relationships were lapsed? Developing and keeping relationships is not only for those who are natural at schmoozing. It is a learned skill that can be done in a number of different ways. Whole books have been written on the subject, but I want to suggest a practical system, modified from a process taught to me by one of my earlier mentors.

Measure the strength of your personal network.

The whole objective of networking is to expand your contact list in two ways: increase the number of relationships, and increase the quality of those relationships. Obviously, this cannot continue indefinitely – your time is finite, after all – so the challenge is to keep as many balls in the air as possible, keeping the most important relationships strongest, and the less important ones less so.

One of the less-well-known capabilities of Microsoft Outlook[7] is the ability to flag a follow-up date for a contact. You select a contact and choose "Follow-up..." from the Actions menu. Then choose a date. Here's how the networking system works:

7. Microsoft Outlook is one of the most popular email, calendar, and contact management programs; it shouldn't be confused with Microsoft's Outlook Express, a different, far more limited program. While the instructions given in this section are specific to Outlook, they can be adapted to the many other contact management programs that are available.

1. The beginning part of every day is spent "processing" your follow-ups.
2. For each follow-up contact, send them something in the postal mail, or send them something via email, or leave them a voice-message about something, or call them about something.

   What is the "something"? That depends on their interests. Here are some examples:

   - Consider subscribing to a number of business magazines; after reading the issue, tear out articles that might be of interest to people in your network and send those articles out to them. Rather than spending the time writing a letter, staple your business card to the article, and write a brief "FYI"-type note directly on the card.
   - Send them a birthday or similar "congratulations" card.
   - Take a relevant link from a web site that they wouldn't see themselves and send it via email.
   - Electronically send them a white paper that you wrote.
   - Leave them a voice message pointing them to something relevant, without creating the obligation for them to return your call.
   - Call them about getting together for breakfast, lunch, a sporting event, or something similar, to reconnect.
   - Call them to offer "extra" tickets for a sporting event or a symphony performance.
   - There is no limit to what you can do; it's limited only by how much you know about their interests.

     Important: Never, ever, send something that looks like a form letter. Never, ever, send email "bulk" to a number of people at once, either visibly with cc's, or invisibly with bcc's. Each one must look, and be, completely personal and individualized.

3. After sending the item out or making the phone call, record the event (date and what was sent or said) in the contact notes area in Outlook; then set the next follow-up date. Depending on how strong the relationship is, set the follow-up date to either 12 months, 3 months, 6 weeks, or 4 weeks. In rare cases, you might want to remove someone completely from the follow-up schedule. Clearly, the stronger the relationship, the faster the cycle the person would be on.

Never send "bulk" emails to your contacts.

4. How to start: If they aren't there already, add each of the 150 "natural market" contacts into your Outlook Contact list. (If you have not left the Mother Ship yet, make sure the contacts are added on your personal, non-work computer.) Now go through the list one by one, and set follow-up dates. Try to spread out the initial follow-up dates so that you don't have a big "lump" of work to do when that date comes around. If you have an excessive number of contacts, start with your highest priority contacts first.

How many contacts might this work for? On average if your contacts are on a three-month rotation (i.e., 60 business days), and you "send out" 15 things each day, then you can manage a network 900 people strong. This is far more than the 150 names we discussed earlier in the chapter! The math is actually quite alluring: if you send or call only three contacts daily, an exceptionally low number, with an average three-month rotation, you can manage a 180-person network.

The system helps keep the relationship alive through the value that you add; when you need their help, or when they need yours, the relationship investment will pay off.

Leverage Strengths

Industry

If it looks like you will stay in the same industry, what can you do to increase your profile there, while you are still with your current employer? There are a number of opportunities, including the following:

Start something that moves you forward toward your goals.

- Being a delegate on a standard-setting body.
- Providing input to regulatory authorities.
- Volunteering in your industry association.
- Teaching a course on your industry at a college or vocational school.
- Writing articles for your trade magazine.
- Public speaking in your field.

Personal Characteristics

What is it that really has accounted for your success so far? All the diagnostics that you did earlier (SkillChecks, Reality Check Interviews, etc.) should point you in the right direction. Until you leave, what can you do to further reinforce these strengths? Perhaps there is a way to become publicly recognized for them. Look at the industry list (above) for a few ideas. While there may not be that much time to do anything substantial, the main point is to start something that moves you forward toward your goals.

Deal with Weaknesses

Strengthen Your Weaknesses

After a certain point in our career, we often convince ourselves that more progress can be made by focusing on our strengths and ignoring our weaknesses. While this is true when you're surrounded by elaborate support structures, it isn't exactly true if you've decided to strike out on your own. In fact, the difference between success and failure may depend precisely on how you perform in those areas that are your blind spots.

In high school, what was the one subject you didn't like and avoided as much as possible? Ask yourself today if you feel the same way about the subject, and indeed how much you are currently using those skills. For myself, I dropped physical education as soon as I could, partly because of the demotivating teachers I had, but mostly because I was uncoordinated and not "jock" material. Today, I go to the gym 12 to 16 hours each week, am very fit, and have earned a Black Belt in karate. For you, perhaps you have begun to be more interested in history, religion, genealogy, or as I have, in fitness. The point: perspective comes with maturity and experience; a weakness of ten years ago may have caused you to artificially close the door on your development in this area. The "old" weakness lives only in your mind, and not in reality!

Notwithstanding this logic, let us not have the weakness of arrogance: we all have our strengths, and we all have our weaknesses. These weaknesses can be categorized three ways: Skills, Industry, and Personal Style weaknesses.

SKILLS WEAKNESS: I don't enjoy the accounting or bookkeeping function, so why bother investing in making me better at something I really will always avoid? No doubt, we have all felt this way about certain parts of our jobs at one point, but if you are leaving the Mother Ship, you must look at your *skill weaknesses* through a wider lens. Perhaps, in your new venture, you will not be able to afford an accountant on day one. Or maybe you are moving into a senior role where you have oversight of the accounting and financial functions. Learning to "speak the language" of accounting and financial analysis may be critical to communicating with functional experts in this area.

Here are some ideas on how to improve your skills knowledge:

- **Take an introductory course.** A number of courses are offered by colleges, private training academies, professional trade groups, etc., that are relatively low cost and relatively high quality. Taking a course provides the extra benefit of giving you a built-in network of those within the field already.

- **Hire a tutor.** For a fairly low cost, you can hire a person to buff up specific areas of weakness. The extra benefit of hiring a tutor is that you can call on them for help later, if you find yourself stuck.
- **Sign up for a degree program or a professional designation.** Whether or not you decide to complete an MBA, a CFA, or some other acronym, the course work required is usually intense, relevant, and valuable. Be realistic, however, about how much time you can devote to actually completing the course of studies. The objective here is to improve a weakness, not earn the degree.[8]
- **Arrange for your next assignment at your current workplace to include elements of the skills you wish to develop.** For example, if you have identified project management as a weakness, choosing an assignment where these skills must be developed properly, and delivered by you personally, will absolutely ensure that you develop the skills!
- Again, in the context of your current position, put yourself in a position to **manage those with the specific skills that you are weak in.** Get yourself trained as the "back-up" for your staff.

INDUSTRY WEAKNESS: Perhaps your next move is to an industry where your knowledge, however strong, is from the perspective of an outsider. While the specifics of how to close this gap would be unique to your situation, here are a few ideas that can help:

- **Trade journals:** Read the last five years' issues, then subscribe to all the trade journals yourself. Old issues are usually available free of charge in the larger city (and college) reference libraries, and sometimes on-line. If your current employer has a library, check there as well. The paper version, with all the advertising included, is likely to be more helpful.

---

8. But if you are taking a number of courses, you may as well earn the degree or certification anyway!

- **Industry research:** Arrange to get industry research from investment banks and brokers for your "target" industry. Usually they write shorter analysis for retail investors, and comprehensive, complete analysis for institutional investors. This latter type of research is often difficult to come by, but when available, is excellent.
- **Newsletters:** There are a number of web-based and email-based newsletters and discussion groups; some of these have dozens (or hundreds) of submissions daily, and most of them are available at low or no cost. If there is a digest option, be sure to choose it, otherwise your email box may be inundated with individual messages. Make the newsletters part of your daily reading regime.
- **Commissioned research:** Pay an MBA student to do a "survey" on the industry you are considering, addressing the industry structure, issues, trends, and key success factors. (You can also consider journalism students.)
- **Gurus:** After becoming reasonably familiar with the industry, purchase two to three hours of time from an industry guru, to validate your understanding of the issues facing the industry. Gurus can come from many places: the publisher of a trade magazine, the financial analyst who has covered the sector for 20 years, the entrepreneur who has "struck it big" more than once, a college professor whose research concentration is in the area, etc.
- **Jobs:** Take a part-time job in the industry. Live the dream, and learn the industry.
- **Reality Check interviewees:** Spend more time with one of the people you interviewed for your Reality Check. Particularly if they have experience in your area of weakness, time with them can be invaluable.

PERSONAL STYLE WEAKNESSES: Arrogant, overeager, too quiet, a push-over, crude, sexist, racist, binary, impatient, too forgiving, too aggressive, meek, headstrong, patronizing, insincere. This list of ugly descriptors, unfortunately, can go on for pages.

Understanding your *personal style* weaknesses is sometimes a bit touchy, as we each tend to think of ourselves as having "great" – or at least not deficient – personal style. The truth, however, is that it is hard to see ourselves properly in the mirror. Small things that we say can create great dysfunction, and we remain unaware and oblivious. Other behaviors we obsess about, yet they are not important at all. Sometimes, we feel that we don't have a "problem," but perceptions effectively become reality, and therefore still must be identified and addressed.

A good third-party diagnostic is critical. Thankfully, there are at least two that should be easily available: your prior personnel reviews, and the findings from the Reality Check Interviews, completed earlier.

- **Personnel interviews:** The first step is to get copies of your last five written reviews – something often easier said than done. Re-read these reviews, but instead of remembering the good times (or "that awful manager"), pay close attention to comments that speak to any style weaknesses. Sometimes code words are used, obscuring the real meaning. For example, if you are described as being a "strong advocate of his own views," perhaps it really means that you tend not to listen well and have a big mouth. Write down all hints of style weaknesses; identification and acknowledgment are the first step to dealing with them.
- **Reality Check Interviews:** While most of these interviews focus on the interviewee, some of the common themes will likely relate to your strengths and weaknesses.

Changing personal style is just about the toughest task you can do. It may also be close to impossible. Nevertheless, sometimes an investment here pays dividends well beyond your job. (Think about your relationships with your spouse and kids.) A rational question would be "What is reasonable to achieve?" It is unlikely that a "softie" can be quickly changed into an "SOB" overnight, or vice-versa. Indeed, your particular skills, *including your weaknesses,* have played an important role in your success to date.

A more practical, and reasonable, approach is to look at your personal style, and then commit to developing a greater *flexibility* of style. If you were able to change your approach to suit the style of the person or groups that you interact with, then that would be a major leap forward. Consider: when a team is behind schedule, is it better to browbeat them with pressure, or "buck them up" with encouragement? Each of us as managers has a more comfortable zone of style; in order to develop flexibility, the task is to consider what other types of responses will achieve the same desired goal. Said another way, consider responses other than what usually first comes out of your mouth. At the end of the day, you may do exactly what you had first thought of, but sometimes, you will react differently – and that is the beginning of style flexibility.

Commit to developing a greater *flexibility* of style.

We probably should look at something about another personal style weakness: bad habits. If you have them, you must stop them. The list of annoying habits can be endless – for example, everyone has one colleague who doesn't stop picking their nose or teeth, fiddles with their watch, always answers their cell phones during meetings, or is constantly jingling the coins in their pockets. For many, smoking falls into this bad habit category as well. In your current relatively senior position, those around you (and especially your subordinates) usually will tolerate these habits, but when you have left the Mother Ship, you may find that prospective clients and partners are far less forgiving.

Whether it is a weakness in personal style, or "just" an annoying habit, here are several ideas that may help:

- Acknowledge your weaknesses and bad habits to yourself by writing them down. Then rank the top three attitudes or behaviors you wish to change. Before you begin each work day, remind yourself of them.
- Prior to reacting with your "gut," put yourself in the other person's shoes, and ask yourself what you could say that would yield the desired result.
- Get a family member, co-worker, or trusted subordinate to give you a private signal whenever the habit shows up.

- Leverage any workplace-provided Employee Assistance Programs for counseling and suggestions.
- Like Rome, your style wasn't built in a day. Recognize that it will take more than a day to change it.

Leaving Your Weaknesses as Is

Perhaps you've buttressed your weaknesses as much as possible, or perhaps time hasn't permitted as much work on your weaknesses as you'd like. There still remains a question: will the sum total of your weaknesses increase your future risks beyond what is acceptable? If the answer is no, then no problem. Remain aware of your weaknesses, but spend your time on other activities. If the weaknesses are relevant to your next position, the only way to address them is to hire (or partner with) someone whose strengths are exactly your weaknesses.

Avoid Planning Paralysis

Plan plan plan plan Plan plan plan plan Plan plan plan plan Plan plan plan plan Plan plan plan plan Plan plan plan plan Plan plan plan plan Plan plan plan plan Plan plan plan plan Plan plan plan plan Plan plan plan plan Plan plan plan plan Plan plan plan plan Plan plan plan plan Plan plan plan plan Plan plan plan plan Plan plan plan plan Plan plan plan plan Plan plan plan plan Plan plan **act!** plan Plan plan plan plan Plan plan plan plan Plan plan plan plan Plan plan plan plan Plan plan plan plan Plan plan plan plan Plan plan plan plan

Get it? Too much planning, too little action! There are many reasons why we plan so much. Do any of these sound familiar?

- **INERTIA:** We've always done it that way.
- **FEAR OF RISK OR FEAR OF FAILURE:** Sometimes we think it makes sense to plan out all the possibilities, just so we will know what to do in every conceivable scenario.
- **FEAR OF THE UNKNOWN:** Sometimes planning takes the place of action because we're uncertain of what the future

may hold. We procrastinate, instead of jumping in the water and learning to swim.

- **COMFORT IN BUSYWORK:** With so much to do before actually leaving…

Interestingly, in the software development world, there are two different philosophies for delivering a project. In "RAD" – Rapid Application Development – a working prototype is built and tested, and then users provide feedback, which then gets incorporated into a second prototype. Users provide more feedback, which gets incorporated into a third prototype, and so on. The development project is completed when the feedback suggests that it is "ready" for production. In the other approach, called "Waterfall," a Requirements Document is produced and then signed off by the user community. Then a Functional Specification is produced and signed off. Then a Technical Specification is produced and signed off. Then development starts. Once complete, it is tested, bugs fixed, then "accepted" by the users for production.

Plan! act! plan! act! plan! act! act! act! plan! act! act! act! plan! act! act! act!

While technology folks will tell you that there are plenty of problems with RAD, it does have two appealing benefits: many opportunities for mid-course corrections, and stuff that is produced right from the start. The problem with the Waterfall approach is that when the development phase is complete and the project deployed, users' requirements may have changed dramatically from when the plan was originally agreed to.

When *you* spend so much time planning, rather than acting, your requirements may have changed too. And even if they haven't, with all your attention on planning for the perfect scenario, you may miss an obvious triggering event for an even better scenario.

Another perspective on planning vs. action is the law of diminishing marginal returns. It is often simplified to the neat equation of 20% of the effort for 80% of the result. This makes sense, in that most people are not interested in the other side of the equation, which is spending 80% of the effort for a mere 20% of the result.

How does this jibe with concepts such as RAD and continuous improvement? Once the 80% result is complete, then that is precisely the time to look around, check your compass, and possibly do a mid-course correction. At this point, the process can start again, with 20% effort giving us another 80% result. Assuming no mid-course correction, you will now be at a 96% result. And the cycle can continue, until you are at the point where it really doesn't matter about the marginal improvement.

Planning is important, but action is better.

In the context of filling in the gaps, what if the triggering event occurs earlier than you expect it to? Having spent only 20% of the time doing 80% of the preparation reduces your risk considerably. And having opportunities to do a mid-course correction after spending only 20% of your effort isn't so bad either. While planning is important, action is better.

"Start" the Business

Prepare Your Résumé

The first thing that needs to be done is to update your résumé. There are dozens of books and many on-line resources that can help you do this. Doing your résumé is important, even if you are not looking for a traditional job. Once again, it helps solidify your skills and accomplishments, at least in your mind. It pulls your experience together in a format that is designed to communicate and to sell.

Instead of merely taking your old résumé and updating your most recent accomplishments or positions, consider rewriting it from scratch, with the aim of making it reflect your target interest. For example, if you are a CFO looking for a general management position, the résumé should reflect your broad experience, and not just your financial acumen. If you are an executive looking to become an entrepreneur, the résumé should reflect the risk-taking entrepreneurial nature of your past assignments.

You may also wish to make a second "mini-bio" version of your résumé, which reflects your experience in two to three paragraphs. Imagine that someone is reading this mini-bio as an introduction to a speech you are giving.

Once the résumé and the mini-bio are done, they can be used in just about any situation you find yourself in: for prospective employers, as a calling card for recruiters, as an insert into a business plan, as part of a brochure or web site, or in a consulting proposal.

Write a Business Plan

A formal *business* plan may not be necessary if you are looking to move into a corporate setting, but a plan is still necessary. Who are your target companies? How will you contact them? Will you be using any of the web-based job boards? Will you use a recruiter (and which one)? What quotas will you set for yourself with regard to networking? What compensation package would be optimal? What is the minimum you would be prepared to accept? Contingency plans: what if you can't find exactly what you're looking for?

How widely you share the plan will depend on your chosen option.

If you are looking to reduce your work week, stay at home, or do something non-traditional, it still makes sense to commit to a plan. What changes will you have to make? What specific objectives are you committing yourself to? What might you do afterwards?

For just about any other option, a more traditional business plan is a must. How widely you share the plan will depend on your chosen option. In some cases, it means using the plan to present to investors; in other cases, it may mean showing it only to a few close confidantes. While there are many books (and online resources) that can help you to write your plan, the basic outline should address the following topics:

BUSINESS DESCRIPTION AND STRATEGY: What is the business's purpose, and how will it be achieved? What is the business model? How is the strategy unique and sustainable?

FINANCIAL: What is the ownership structure? Where is the money coming from, and where will it be spent? You need to include three years of financial projections and sensitivity analysis, along with supporting assumptions.

MARKETING: Describe the marketing processes, including branding, partnerships, advertising, direct mail, Internet. Who are the competitors, and how is the enterprise differentiated?

SALES: Describe the sales channels, strategies, and the sales process. Describe any existing "pipeline," and the assumptions supporting the sales forecast.

OPERATIONS: Describe how the product is produced, inventoried, and shipped. If you will be providing a service, describe the methodology. Describe R&D plans, including any unique intellectual property.

HUMAN RESOURCES: Include mini-bios of all key executives. Describe unique HR policies and plans. Describe your role in detail.

Many other sections can be added to a business plan, depending on the situation. Feel free to be creative, but do spend the time putting at least something down on paper, no matter what your chosen option. Writing it down gives you, yet again, the opportunity to fine-tune your decision.

Administration and Logistics

When the time comes to actually jump, all your attention should be on the opportunity itself. Don't be distracted by administration and logistics. To give you this focus, there are a number of things to review and address beforehand:

Your Rights and Obligations

When you started your current job, you may have signed an employment agreement that imposed specific obligations on you and your employer. An employment agreement, however, is not the only place that rights and obligations are defined. For example, obligations may be embedded in an employment application that you signed dozens of years ago, or in confidentiality agreements that you sign annually. You may implicitly agree to other obligations (and give up certain rights) when you log on to an email system or intranet. Obligations are also derived from employment law.

Employment law varies by jurisdiction. At one extreme, many American states have "employment at will" laws, by which employees can quit (or be fired) with no notice, obligation, or severance. At the other extreme, some Canadian provinces and some European countries are slanted so far in the employees' favor that it is almost impossible to fire an employee, except at great cost. Often, the statute law mandates certain minimums with respect to severance, notice, and employment conditions. Common law (i.e., the body of law derived from court rulings) usually extends legislation considerably.

Understand your legal and contractual position.

Whether because of the law, your company's policies, or an explicit employment agreement, there are a number of areas you should clarify before you leave. Since every situation is unique, make sure to hire legal counsel to advise you on the specifics of your circumstances.

SEVERANCE: If you leave on your own accord, what severance, if any, is payable?

NOTICE: How much notice must you give your employer, according to the letter of your agreement? If your agreement is silent on this, what is the minimum length of notice you are required to give, by law? What is the length of notice you *should* give to allow an orderly transfer of responsibility and to maintain a friendly relationship? Can you give notice at any time of the year, or is there a particular time when you must give notice (e.g., 30 days prior to a contract anniversary or at the end of a project)?

NON-COMPETE: Are you restricted from competing with your employer in any way? Be sure to get legal advice if you have restrictions and if your next role might be considered competition. Courts sometimes strike down clauses with unreasonably broad restrictions.

NON-SOLICITATION: Once you leave, are you restricted in any way from contacting or soliciting current or past customers? Are you restricted in any way from hiring (or even providing a reference for) your former colleagues?

INTELLECTUAL PROPERTY RIGHTS: Have you given to your current employer any and all intellectual property rights to everything you were involved in while employed? Or did you retain some degree of ownership? If you developed a process or methodology while with your current employer, could you use the same process with your new employer? Do you have any right to keep any of your correspondence and files? If yes, when you do move to your new position, what steps must you take to make sure you are not sued for intellectual property infringement? If your manager allows you to take certain files, for example, make sure you get written permission to do so. If a legal issue comes up several years later and your manager is unavailable (or forgetful), written documentation will solve many problems for you.

REIMBURSED EXPENSES AND ACCRUALS: At what point can the company stop paying your expenses: at the time of notice, your last day on the job, or at some later time? Medical bills or insurance fees, for example, may come due after you have left, but may relate to services performed while you were an employee. You may find that certain benefits (such as life insurance) may continue for a period of time beyond the termination of your employment.

Pay particular attention to any vacation accruals you have earned over your entire career with your employer. While company policy may say "use it or lose it," this may actually be contrary to legislation in your jurisdiction. Upon your departure, you may be entitled to a substantial accrued vacation payment. Once again, a good employment lawyer could be able to help.

TIMING ISSUES AND THE COST OF LEAVING: Depending on when (and how) you leave, what happens to your stock options, warrants, restricted stock, or other equity participation? Do you lose anything that is not yet vested? Do you have a certain amount of time to exercise any vested options or warrants after you've departed, or do they all expire immediately? Make sure that you see a copy of the policy in writing, prior to making any decisions. A question answered verbally by someone without the authority to answer could cost you dearly if they are wrong.

Similarly, there is an issue of the status of commissions, bonuses, deferred compensation, and pension benefits. Can the value of these be maximized by slightly adjusting the timing of your departure?

It would be worthwhile to understand your employer's policy and practice on these issues. Official policies might help, but also consider discussing your situation with others who have left the organization in the past.

Speak to others who have left.

CLAW-BACKS: Are there any expenses (clubs memberships, medical expenses, conference fees, training expenses, etc.) that the company will expect you to pay back on your leaving, either in full or *pro rata?* Often this is a bit of a surprise, as one's final pay may be substantially lower (or negative!) as a result of these claw-backs.

Benefits

Evaluate your entire benefits package for portability. For example, life insurance can usually be purchased by an employee on termination of employment without evidence of good health, so long as it is done within a set period of time. If you have a health problem, you may not be able to get life insurance privately, nor at your new position. If this is the case, buying out your current group policy, at any cost, may be worthwhile. Before you do it, though, review your entire insurance plan with a trusted insurance professional.

Don't forget to review your benefit plan to ensure that you have taken advantage of all the benefits that are available to you. You may as well have your dental work taken care of (or new eyeglasses purchased) with a plan that you know. In fact, if your plan "pre-pays" for benefits, you are effectively losing your own money if you do not use up the benefits before you leave.[9]

Maxing out on your benefits is particularly important if you are moving to a situation where they are not provided. Be careful, though, if your current employer has "claw-back" policies.

9. Prepaid health benefits are sometimes known as *health spending accounts.*

Infrastructure

Since it is inappropriate to work on your business during the day, you need to set up a proper office at home. While you probably have one already, it is likely more suited to occasional work-from-home or personal activities such as bill-paying. At the outset, "Filling in the Gaps" is a full-time job, on top of your current day-job responsibilities; you will need an appropriate place to do the work. If possible, the location of the office should be private enough to allow you to concentrate without interruptions.

The list below is a good starting point for some of the equipment you'll likely need. How much you invest in a home office while you are filling in the gaps is dependent on what you eventually will be doing. A free agent's needs will be very different than if you're hoping to trade up to a corporate position elsewhere.

- Computer (preferably a laptop).
- Software for office productivity, anti-virus, and back-up.
- Second phone line.
- Fax machine.
- Office-quality printer.
- High-speed Internet (e.g., cable or DSL broadband).
- File cabinet for business correspondence.
- Office-quality voicemail.
- Cell phone.
- Office supplies.
- Shredder.
- Private workplace (e.g., not the kitchen table).

To repeat once again: it is not acceptable to be using your employer's supplies, equipment, or premises to do your personal administration and logistics. Besides being morally wrong, you are effectively stealing your employer's resources; if things suddenly take a turn for the worse, there is a risk of dismissal with cause. The risk to your reputation isn't worth it.

In case you are *still* thinking of using your employer's infrastructure, consider the following:

- Your current emails can be retrieved from the server. Your emails from the last few years are typically backed up and can also be retrieved on demand. Every one of your emails can be read as they are sent or received.
- If you delete files on your computer, they can be undeleted. Even files that are months (or years) old can usually be retrieved.
- All web-based email (such as Hotmail) that you send or receive from your computer can be copied and archived.
- All web sites that you look at can be logged.
- All of the above documents can be indexed and searched electronically to bring up references to a specific word or company name.
- Old voicemail messages can be retrieved, even if you personally deleted them.

To repeat: do your personal business on your personal equipment, at home.

Business Registration

If you have decided to do anything that involves setting up a company, you will have to satisfy various government registration requirements. Some of the registration is for the rights to the name, other requirements are for legal or taxation purposes.

Having a discussion with legal and tax experts at an early stage may make a difference down the line. Keep a number of considerations in mind:

- What is the most tax-efficient form of business structure for the enterprise to take, and should it take that form at the very beginning? (e.g., should it be incorporated right from the start?)
- Should ownership be split with family members, for income-splitting and estate-planning purposes? If yes, what protective clauses should be in a shareholder agreement?

- If there is an R&D component to the business, does offshore ownership of the intellectual property make sense?

Separate from the business registration itself is the purchase of an Internet domain name (in the case of this book, leavingthemothership.com). With the domain name, you can then later set up a web site and email addresses.

Banking

After registering your business with the appropriate authorities, you will be able to open a bank account. Having a strong relationship with your banker is critical; when a banker is making a decision, in addition to using their financial analysis, more often than not their judgment will also be part of the process.

One executive who left a senior position at a multibillion-dollar enterprise to advise a newly public company ran into an interesting situation. Calling his contacts at one of the major banks to enquire about setting up a small line of credit for the business, he was informed that his contact dealt only with credit lines over $100 million. He needed less than $5 million. Despite the humor of the situation, the relationship provided a valuable entrée!

There is a definite benefit to setting up your banking as early as possible. To combat fraud, many banks routinely place "holds" on funds deposited to new customers' accounts. The earlier you establish an account, the earlier these restrictions are removed and the earlier you develop a corporate credit rating. Opening a business account also avoids the record-keeping problem of mingling personal and business funds.

Professional Services

BOOKKEEPING AND ACCOUNTING: From the very start of your efforts, you will likely be incurring *bona fide* expenses. Some costs might be those related to your home office, others might be for professional services (e.g., legal and accounting) while others might be related to marketing and sales.

Your accountant can help you define a mechanism to capture these expenses as they are being incurred. They can also help determine what computer software to use, how to set up a chart of accounts, and whether you should do the bookkeeping yourself or outsource it.

Every jurisdiction has different rules on the deductibility of expenses, particularly for home offices, cars, meals, and entertainment. Get professional advice about which expenses are allowable and which aren't, so that you won't be unpleasantly surprised after the fact.

LEGAL ADVICE: When you visit a bookstore, you will be amazed at the number of books that provide pseudo-legal advice: from incorporating your own company, to providing "standard" contract forms, to filing trademarks, to filing lawsuits. If you are even thinking of relying on these generalized how-to guides for your legal needs, don't. These guides might not take into account the specifics of common law in your jurisdiction. They might not be up-to-date. And they certainly don't take into account anything particular about your situation. The bookstore guides can be useful, though, for a different reason. They will teach you the lingo and help you advise your legal counsel more effectively.

You will definitely need professional legal advice when something goes wrong. And when that happens, you want to make sure you have covered yourself properly, which can happen only if your contracts are written correctly, right from the start.

Dealing with professionals must be done in as efficient a manner as possible, or else fees will become an issue, along with questions of their value. One way of enhancing efficiency is to ensure that they are focused on providing legal advice. This means providing your lawyer with a "term sheet" that should form the basis of a contract, rather than having your lawyer (and the counterparty's lawyer) haggle over business terms.[10] Another way is to ask your lawyer to provide template contracts

10. Of course, some lawyers provide business advisory services as well, often assisting in business negotiation. If this is how you are using your lawyer, no problem, but be aware that this is what you are doing.

that can be used for various purposes with minimal changes (e.g., employment contracts, confidentiality agreements, vendor contracts). Too many businesses write new contracts for each deal they do.

Whether it is your lawyer, accountant, or another professional you are dealing with, make sure you understand the basis of their fees. No one likes a surprise.

Corporate Identity

While less relevant if you are going the corporate route, developing a brand and an identity is important for all businesses. Presumably, you already have a business name and have now secured (and protected) your rights to use it. Instead of spending money at the local photocopy shop getting cheapo business cards and stationery, engage a professional graphic designer to develop your corporate identity. This may include a logo, stationery, and business cards. Even if you are looking to move to another corporate job, having a *personal* identity that looks professional can pay back handsomely.

If the designer has experience, they will also be able to design a PowerPoint presentation template and a simple web site. (The web site can always be enhanced once you have your enterprise under way.) These simple investments, which you will have to make anyway, lend important credibility, especially at the beginning.

One young entrepreneur, selling his services to a multinational, had his business cards printed with the title "Sales Manager." Asked why he did this, rather than having the title of "President" or "Managing Director," he responded that having a less senior title meant that his customers would assume there was significant infrastructure behind him. And, he continued, since he looked so young, having a senior title would give him less credibility than a junior one. Whether this applies in your situation or not, the story illustrates the importance of attention to detail when it comes to your identity, and its impact.

Before printing business cards, make sure you arrange for your "new" email address. It is very important not to use AOL, Hotmail, or other generic services for email, as these generic services lack credibility: use *your* new domain name.

Often people who spend many years at the same organization have thoroughly mixed their personal and professional lives. This is especially evident in their email correspondence. As soon as possible, you should set up a separate *personal* email address (separate from your "new" corporate one), then advise your family and long-time friends to send personal email there. If your corporate email gets cut off unexpectedly, at least you won't lose your personal network.

Separate your personal and professional lives.

At this point, you should have three email addresses: one from your current employer, accessed only from your current employer's computer; a second one you've set up for your new operation; and a third one you've set up for personal correspondence. Tip: most email programs can be configured to check *both* new email addresses automatically, simplifying life for you significantly.

KEY POINTS

Using your time productively in the time between your decision to go and your eventual departure is critical. Keep your focus, and avoid busywork and procrastination.

ACTION CHECKLIST

- ❑ Labeling exercise
- ❑ Personal Balance Sheet action plans
- ❑ Personal networking
- ❑ Address your weaknesses
- ❑ Prepare your résumé (and if applicable, your business plan)
- ❑ Administration and logistics of your departure
- ❑ Administration and logistics of setting up your new enterprise

Chapter 12: Making the Jump

Triggering Events

Being prepared is one thing, but knowing exactly when to jump is another. Consider re-reading the section on triggering events. As you have refined your direction considerably since triggering events were introduced, you should have some ideas as to what the likely triggers would be for your particular situation.

Write them down! Challenge yourself; if you come up with ten potential triggering events, try to add five others. Of course, *the* trigger may eventually be very different from any of these. The trigger may come at the most unexpected time, but by writing down a list of potential ones, you will at least be sensitized to their possibility.

Severance

When a company is looking to reduce employee headcount, they will often offer generous severance packages to those they wish to let go. Less frequently, a company may offer a general package that anyone who fits into a particular category may choose to accept. For example, older employees, who are often more costly than their younger peers, may be asked to consider early retirement and would be given a severance sweetener to make it appealing.

I'm a star. Is severance really possible?

The question at hand is simple: is it at all possible, as a star performer who wishes to leave, to approach your employer and get them to agree to a generous severance? To answer this question, you must first understand how your employer would see your request. From their perspective…

- They really enjoy working with you – so why pay you to go?
- They don't relish the time and cost of finding your replacement – so why invite the extra expense and hassle?
- They see your unique value that you add to the organization – so why pay you to go?

- Your high salary and years of service translate into an expensive severance – so why volunteer to pay it?
- If you are going to leave anyway – why incur the expense voluntarily?
- They know that your employment contract specifies no severance at all in case of a voluntary departure – so no matter the above, there aren't any legal obligations to pay.

Tough questions all! But there is hope. Unfortunately, the downside to even approaching the issue is that you will have to share some of your thinking about leaving the organization. And this may mean that your plans could be accelerated at a faster rate than you expected. As a result, you may not have enough time to fill in the gaps properly. And you will have introduced new worries to your employer: how much can you be trusted, and what if you leave before a replacement can be found?

Your plans should be set well before you get your severance – not afterwards.

Many years ago I felt this worry acutely. Staying late one night, I went to the printer to retrieve some correspondence. On the printer tray was my letter, but also a copy of a key employee's résumé. I had no idea this employee was looking to leave, and I was completely shocked to find the résumé there. I didn't say anything to the person, but I did take steps to protect the company in case the person gave unexpected notice. In the end, the person stayed for 18 more months before moving on. The worry was very, very real.

If you think you can get a large severance payment, and then use the breathing space to figure out what you are going to do, think again. Your plans should be set well before you get your severance – not afterwards. If and when the golden handshake comes, you should already be in the sprint.

So how might you precipitate a severance offer? Here are some ideas:

- **GIVE LESS EFFORT.** As an executive, when they "buy" you, they are buying 120% of your time and effort. Nights, weekends, breakfast, lunch, and dinner. It doesn't usually specify this in your employment contract in so many words, but for most star managers and executives, this is an unwritten part of the deal. If your employer knows you will not be putting in this extra effort, they may believe that you will not be able to do the full job. While this in itself might not suddenly get you a severance package, it still can be a plank in your arguments with them.

One manager had spent ten years helping to build the back office of his company's stock brokerage operation. When the company was acquired, he faced a choice: either continue his 120% effort (as many of his colleagues did), or merely do an "honest day's work" and be targeted for a package. His decision was difficult, as he was used to being involved in most management decisions; just doing an "honest day's work" meant toning down his contribution significantly.

He reduced his work effort to 100% and spent the extra time investing in himself: filling in the gaps for an eventual departure. In this particular case, he would have left on his own at some point anyway; the acquisition of his employer was merely the triggering event that propelled him to action. In the end, he was offered a generous severance.

An orderly handover is impossible if your departure is a surprise.

- **TAKE ADVANTAGE OF YOUR EMPLOYER'S WORRIES.** From an employer's perspective, there is a terrible risk that you will leave at a critical time, perhaps during contract negotiations, or maybe just prior to a crucial sales meeting. Furthermore, the question of an orderly handover to your successor is pretty much impossible if your departure is a surprise to them. This is probably your strongest argument for a mutually agreed release. Your agreement to stay until a certain period of time (project completion, successor trained, deal negotiated, etc.) may be worth far more to your employer than even the most generous severance package. Part of your severance may even include a consulting services contract for a period of time to reduce their risks further.

In this particular case, the conversation might unfold over several meetings. Tell them you are looking to understand your next career step within the organization. Let them know that you don't see where your place could possibly be. Probe to see if there is even the mildest buy-in for this idea, and let your employer know that the prospect of moving on, while a bit scary, would be something you would consider seriously. Give your employer time to reflect on what you've said; they might come up with ideas you hadn't previously considered. Let them know, however, that there is a deadline: you're looking to define whether your next step is inside or outside by a certain date.

- **WORK YOURSELF OUT OF A JOB.** If your project is finished, or if you have delegated all your value-added responsibilities to others, your employer may consider your "offer" to quit with severance as a great way to reduce overheads. This approach has the added value of saying to your manager: "Letting me go reduces your overhead." This strategy also reduces your manager's worry about succession planning and reduces the time cost (and uncertainty) of your departure.
- **MAKE A "CONSIDERED" ULTIMATUM.** Consider the following scenario: You have been actively courted by others, with compensation offers far higher than your current plan. Industry salary surveys corroborate this. And you know, indisputably, that your colleagues are paid far more than you. What would happen if you brought this to your employer's attention and asked for more?

  If the difference was minimal, say 10 to 15%, this strategy likely wouldn't work at all, as the differences could easily be explained away. If the difference was substantial, say 30 to 50%, it is unlikely that you would get it either, as an increase so high is often considered too far beyond standard policy. If you are lucky enough for them to say yes, then good for you: if you must work, you may as well be paid as much as the market can bear. Start saving for your transition.

  A general rule is that ultimatums don't win you many friends. If you are hoping to have your employer give you a generous severance offer, you must indeed be friendly. Yet in this situation, you have just said, "Pay me or I quit"! What if, instead, you said that without a significant change, you have no choice but to assume the company just doesn't value your contribution, and their refusal to compensate you fairly essentially is the same as their telling you to leave and go elsewhere.

Ultimatums don't win you many friends.

Since it is unlikely they will suddenly hike your compensation to the fair level, their refusal provides the entrée into a discussion of separation terms. No histrionics or threats: just a matter-of-fact discussion on how to do an orderly transition – and the size of your severance payment.

There are two counter-arguments if your employer decides that "your" decision to leave is your business, and therefore no severance would be paid.

1. Keeping your compensation excessively low is constructively the same as their dismissing you, not the other way around.
2. If you were to continue working on your current compensation plan, neither party would be happy. With a mutually agreed severance plan, there would be no surprises as to the timing of your departure, and an orderly succession plan can be put into place.

- **THREATEN.** You've got to be joking. If you think that threats make sense, re-read the section above about the employer's perspective.

Of course, the conversation that you have will be as unique as your individual situation. No matter how the conversation is framed, take care that it is not deemed to be your resignation. This may unwittingly trigger a clause in your employment contract or company policy, and you may find yourself out of a job immediately – with neither notice nor severance.

If you are considering leaving, spend your time filling in the gaps, and move forward. If you are able to get "severance help" from your current employer, then great: but consider it an extra. If all your focus is on gaining a severance package instead of moving on, this opportunism may cost you both time and happiness. Try for it if possible, but put things in perspective: they don't owe you severance at all, and they've got many good reasons for not giving you a thing. Don't be bitter about losing something you never had.

If you are lucky enough to get severance, remember that it is not without cost. Especially if you are looking for another corporate position, being recruited away from your current employer is far easier than looking for a job when you don't have one. If you are "packaged out," you are no different than the legions of other unemployed: this is not a positive way to differentiate yourself at all!

How to Afford It?

While severance certainly can help, one of the questions, no matter the path you choose, is the financial viability of your choice: in other words, how do you afford to do what you want to do? You might be thinking, for example, of the following questions:

- What if I trade up to a bigger company, it doesn't work out, and I'm on the street?
- How can I afford to start a new business; I can't make ends meet as it is!
- What will happen to my house if I can't make the mortgage payments? How can I pay for my vacation/health care/kid's education/etc. if things go wrong?
- etc.
- etc.

The financially toughest of all the options are the ones that are designed to reduce your income: moving to a reduced work week, or taking a leave to raise children or care for elderly parents. Starting a business is also financially tough, as primary funding often will come from...you. Starting a business also means paying yourself less until the business is self-sustaining. Whether you are choosing a corporate move or an entrepreneurial one, or are reducing your income for other reasons, the following suggestions should reduce your stress immeasurably.

Set up a Rainy Day Fund

The concept is simple: save three to six months of income, just in case. If you lose your job, so the theory goes, your rainy day fund can pay expenses until you find your next job.

A rainy day fund provides a safety net and a tremendous psychological boost.

Unfortunately, most people don't have the discipline to save. Those who do have discipline realize that it makes more sense to pay down mortgages and other debt than to keep the rainy day funds in a low-interest-bearing savings account. Nevertheless, if you can save a bit each month, or if you can borrow against your home equity, a rainy day fund provides both the practical advantage of a safety net and a tremendous psychological boost.

A senior sales executive in the high-tech field described the terrible stress he felt each year as the pressure to close deals and meet his quota reached a fever pitch. If he didn't reach high enough, he would get fired, and the prospect of being fired was terrifying. Several years ago, after earning a particularly high commission, he set up a rainy day fund equivalent to three months of salary. He describes his sense of empowerment by the name he chose for the fund: his "F-U" money.

Consider dipping into your rainy day fund during your transition period. For example, if you are moving to another corporate position, maybe the rainy day fund pays for new clothes; maybe it pays for a golf club membership. If you are moving to an entrepreneurial role, the rainy day fund might be used to supplement your salary until the business can stand on its own.

Budgeting

Preparing a detailed personal budget is critical. It may be that you have never needed to budget before, but just as a budget does in business, it embeds a tremendous sensitivity and discipline when you do it personally. From a more practical standpoint, a budget can let you know the size of your financial cushion, and free you from worrying unnecessarily.

Develop the discipline of making, then following a personal budget.

Of course, your budget after the triggering event will be different than your current pattern, both for income and expenses. The objective is to develop the discipline of making, then following a personal budget. Consider the following factors as you prepare your new budget:

SEVERANCE: Have you calculated exactly how much severance you will get from your employer? Don't forget to include accrued vacation pay, bonuses, commissions, expense reimbursement, less any claw-backs. Also, don't forget to consider the *after-tax* amount you will actually receive.

Get your savings working for you.

INCREASE YOUR NON-EMPLOYMENT INCOME: This can mean anything from changing your investment mix to provide more income than capital growth, renting out your cottage or rooms in your house, to sending your spouse "back to work" if he or she doesn't currently work. If you have adult or teenage children whom you are supporting, insist that they contribute to the family finances too.

REDUCE LIVING COSTS: Where does all your money really go? Consider looking at your last three months' expenditures, and categorizing them. What can be deferred until your new position is more certain or your business is on stable ground? What expenses must you really incur at all? Often, we find that our spending has naturally reached the level of available funding. If we reduce the available funding, can our spending be reduced as well?

There are many ways to reduce living costs. Here are a few:

- Eat out less often; when you do eat out, go to less expensive restaurants.
- Postpone expensive vacations.

- Avoid lavish gifts.
- Reduce or eliminate the use of maids, nannies, gardeners, and other helpers.
- Postpone any non-essential expenses for at least three months.
- Start conserving energy around your home.
- Reduce allowances for teenage children, and cut them completely for adult children.
- Do your own laundry, instead of sending it to a service.

If the cash crunch is tough, there are certainly more drastic changes you can make:

- Give up or suspend club memberships.
- Trade in your car for a less expensive one.
- Sell your house and move into a less expensive one.

Be Cheap on Administrative Expenses

Particularly if you have decided to undertake a start-up, each expenditure must go extremely far. Unlike in your soon-to-be corporate past, each expenditure you make should be for something immediately necessary, especially when the spending is on overhead. Shopping at the Big Warehouse for a case of paper clips makes no sense, if a single box of 100 will do you. Don't laugh – I've seen it. (I've also seen cases of paper, cases of pencils, and cases of file folders.)

Every penny saved on overhead ends up in your pocket.

Do you need the absolute latest laptop? The most expensive Palm PDA or cell phone? The fanciest home office desk furniture? Most people go to office supply stores for home office furniture; why not check out second-hand office furniture dealers, where higher quality furniture can be found for a fraction of the price.

Every penny saved on overhead buys you time; every penny saved on overhead ends up in your pocket. If you really want one of those whiz-bang laptops, reward yourself with it when the business can truly afford it. Side benefit: you'll appreciate it more then too.

Seed Capital

Often great ideas are stopped in their tracks because of a roadblock, either real or perceived. The initial capital for an enterprise – seed capital – sometimes fits into this category. Where to find it? Entire books have been written on properly financing your enterprise. The purpose of the list below is to illustrate that there *are* many sources of money, and that these sources are often overlooked.

- General savings.
- Retirement nest egg.
- Second mortgage on house.
- Family and friends.
- Former employer.
- Cash value of life insurance policy.
- Founding clients/Development partners.
- Key suppliers.
- Banks and leasing companies.
- Government grants and loans.
- Angel investors.
- Partners.
- Other financial sources (venture capital companies, merchant banks, etc.).

Telling Your Current Employer

Your good news is very likely their bad news.

Telling your current employer that you will be leaving can be exciting and scary. After all, you have spent many happy productive years there, and leaving, even for a great new position, is bittersweet.

How will the news be taken by those you tell? Your good news is very likely their bad news. Your manager, who is faced with the prospect of replacing an invaluable employee, might feel as if you were leaving the company in the lurch. Your mentors within the organization might feel that your leaving is a repudiation of all their advice, and possibly a betrayal of their trust – especially if you haven't confided in them. And your staff might feel dumped. If the atmosphere (either financial or otherwise) is negative, many of your colleagues might consider whether they should also abandon ship.

Remember that all these people are not privy to the thinking and analysis that you have done to get yourself to this point. Deciding what to tell your current employer is merely a decision of how much of your thinking you wish to share with them. Consider the following conversation, possibly with your manager:

Role-play and rehearse your exit conversation until you are comfortable with it.

> *"I've done some hard thinking about where my career is taking me, and what should be next. I've looked at some of my life priorities and have had to make a number of tough decisions. How much time to spend with my older parents? How much time to spend with my younger children? How much time traveling? What might my next position actually be?*
>
> *"As a result, I am now looking at doing XXXX next. I have looked at the question of how, and have a plan to achieve this goal…*
>
> *"I've had an excellent run here at ABCD co., and the experience gained is what has in fact led to my decision to go. I will miss everyone, but am hoping that we might still find a way to do business together…*
>
> *"Thank you very much for all you have taught me. I will miss our working relationship…*
>
> *"I'm looking to leave within the month. I've got some ideas on how to ensure an orderly transition, and if you like, we can discuss…*
>
> *"Here is my letter of resignation…"*

One of the most important goals of this discussion is to leave on good terms. No matter how much you might despise your manager, hate the organization, and wish to say, "I quit" (or worse), remember that it is a small world indeed. Any ill will that you create will blemish all you have accomplished, and will tarnish your reputation for years.

It is best to be professional, and honestly try to empathize with the feelings of the person you are telling. If your ego or past bad blood makes this especially hard for you, pretend that you will have to call them up the next day in your new role and sell them something. Don't burn your bridges.

Don't burn your bridges.

Your requirements and your employer's are no longer in sync, and by leaving, you are merely recognizing that fact. Convey that you are moving to what is next for you and not running away from them. The name of this book is *Leaving the Mother Ship* – not *Leaving the Sinking Ship*!

In the same way that your employer must be left with the appropriate message, so must your mentors, your staff, and colleagues.

EMPLOYER: You must have agreement with your employer on the timing of your departure, and how they want your time spent until you leave. Is it working on a special project? Documenting your current responsibilities? Working on a transition plan? Or do they wish to walk you out the door immediately? You may have already developed a succession or transition plan, which now only need be implemented.

You must also gain agreement on how your departure will be communicated. Think about offering to write your departure communiqué, to be sent over your manager's signature. Your colleagues must be told, as must your customers and suppliers. Rather than take your chances with a message that might not be to your liking, agree on the protocol for letting each group know.

Do not ask your employer for references, and don't spend your time in the initial meeting negotiating. If you have to do any negotiating, it would be best to let your manager have time to reflect; you wish to avoid a negotiation becoming an argument or grudge match.

Leaving on good terms is important for another reason. For whatever reason, what if you decide that your next move is back to the Mother Ship? Or what if a merger places you there? Several years ago, a new employee joined my group after leaving a competitor. His departure, apparently, was not on the best of terms; in fact, we often heard him deriding his former colleagues. Lo and behold, there was a merger of our parent organizations, and his old group and the current group suddenly became "one." He found himself face-to-face with his former spurned bosses. Needless to say, he didn't last long.

"INTERNAL" MENTORS: You may have included your mentor(s) in your Reality Check Interviews, in which case they know that something may be cooking. Even if you didn't interview them, your relationship may be strong enough that you have already told them anyway. No matter which, it would be wise to alert your mentors first, before you speak to your boss. They may have a perspective that you hadn't considered. For example, they may suggest another opportunity, within the organization, that you hadn't even known about.

Alert your mentors first, before you speak to your boss.

On the other hand, you must decide how much of your mentor's allegiance is to you versus the organization. What might happen if your mentor places the best interests of the organization first, or if they think that your interests really are best served by your staying? You may find yourself in the position of having your manager (and others) learn of your intentions prematurely. And when they find out, they may not hear about the reasons or your willingness to help during the transition. They will only hear that a bomb will soon be dropped. They may even take steps that are designed to protect the enterprise, but end up hurting you.

STAFF AND COLLEAGUES: It is important to speak to your closest staff, including those whom you mentor, in person, and as soon as possible after you speak to your employer. It is a judgment call as to whether you tell your closest confidantes beforehand. In my case, I always did so, but not without risk.

The message for your staff is that your reason for departure relates to your personal goals; it is not about the company and it is certainly not about them. The second message is that there is as much opportunity after your departure as before, and that you are but a phone call away if they need to contact you. You want to let them know how your time will be filled until your departure, and that a transition plan is being worked on.

When I left one of my former employers, I was stunned to find several very senior people asking if I might have a role for them in my new venture. (I didn't.) It seems when you spend the time discussing your personal reasons for doing something, others feel obliged to share their views as well. If someone asks if they could join you after you leave, be careful, especially if you have a non-solicitation clause in your contract. It is probably best to be noncommittal. Tell them you're flattered by their asking and explain to them that your first priority is figuring out the new environment. Tell them that it is really premature to consider anything, and then thank them again. If they are really serious, they will seek you out later.

No matter what your colleagues, staff, mentors, and managers say, they must remember you as a professional, someone with whom they would work again, and whose departure is happening on good terms.

Make the Jump!

When it's time to go, your plan should be pretty much all set. But what if the triggering event happens earlier than you expect it to? You will be miles ahead of the situation where you hadn't done any planning and preparation at all.

And if you have any final doubts, remember: what's the worst thing that can happen? Even if everything fails miserably, no one can say that you didn't have the courage to do it. And you'll be back, with the valuable experience earned only by those who left the Mother Ship.

KEY POINTS

- Keep your eye out for triggering events.
- Severance payments can help, but consider severance a bonus if you are able to get it.
- Financial prudence pays off: start with a rainy day fund, develop a budget, and keep administrative expenses as low as possible.
- Make sure that your mentors are always in the loop.
- Leave your employer on friendly terms: you never know when you will meet them again.

PART III:

Success Beyond the Mother Ship

Congratulations. You are now a full-time stock trader. Or perhaps you have started your own distribution company. Maybe you have left the comfort of being a CFO (or a schoolteacher, or a civil servant) and have the title "President" on your business card for the first time. Whatever you are now doing, you are expecting greater personal fulfillment, financial rewards, and hopefully, better life balance.

While some people are lucky – after all, someone actually does win the lottery – being successful in your new role has very little to do with luck, and very much to do with finding the right opportunity and exploiting it through hard work, the right attitude, and avoiding silly mistakes.

Part III of this book provides perspective: How to avoid common mistakes, and how to do some of the basic things that are so easy to miss.

Chapter 13: Avoiding Common Mistakes

Define Yourself Broadly

Earlier in this book we discussed briefly the problems that can ensue if you have always defined yourself solely in terms of your job. Now that you've left, the problem is no longer merely theoretical: it's real. It *is* really tough to describe yourself in your new role comfortably, especially when you've just started. Here are some suggestions that might make it easier:

1. Strive to describe yourself in non-job terms when outside the workplace. Diversifying yourself to be "more than your job" is critical to achieving balance. Chapter 8 describes ways to do this.
2. When asked directly about your new job, position, or enterprise, answer with a crisp, prepared, memorized response. While it may sound contrived at first, you will quickly develop comfort with the new words.

Dress for Success

How you look makes a big impression on those around you. Especially when you meet someone for the first time, your shoes, clothing, and personal grooming will peg you into a certain category.

As a consultant, the rule has always been to dress just slightly more formally than the client. If you are dressed too casually, you lose credibility. If you are dressed too formally, you appear arrogant. While this rule of thumb seems simple, we ran into an interesting situation with one client. The senior executives all wore suits and ties, but everyone else in the organization wore casual business attire. What to do if you're meeting both in the same day? In this case, we decided we would wear dark blue blazers and white shirts, with an open collar and no tie. When we were with the middle managers, we took off our blazers; when we were with the executives, the jackets stayed on.

How you are perceived makes selling your ideas that much easier.

Why bother paying such close attention to your clothing? Because it is hard enough selling your ideas to others. Paying attention to how you are perceived makes selling your ideas to your colleagues or clients just that much easier.

How different is your new position from your old one? Look in your closet, and make sure that your wardrobe is appropriate given both your new position and the culture of the organization. Several years ago, I found myself promoted from one role to another. One of my staff members was kind enough to point out to me that my clothes must match my new role, not my old one. A bit embarrassing, actually, but very, very helpful.

For those who work from a home office, it is far too easy to amble from your bedroom into the office, wearing only a bathrobe or comfortable lounging clothes. To keep some degree of separation between your home mindset and your work mindset, always dress in appropriate office attire. You'll feel different if you dress for success, whether you're with people at a meeting or on the phone in your office. Postscript: you *can* dress for success and dress for comfort at the same time. If your wardrobe doesn't allow it, go shopping for a wardrobe that does.

Quickly Reset Your Expectations

After so many years on the same ship, your expectations have been well-conditioned to The Way It Is Done. Think about it. How are promotions determined? Are customer policies always tightly enforced, or is there flexibility? Which is more highly valued: getting in early, or staying late? What is the role of a staff department, such as HR, compared to the line manager? How much power is there at the head office compared to those out in the field?

If you are going into another organization, these questions and many others should not be taken for granted. It is better to leave your expectations at the door and approach your new position with an open attitude of learning. Remember, some of your previous success was due to your previous organizational knowledge. Doesn't it make sense to invest time developing knowledge in your "new" organization, before enforcing your assumptions on it? Doing this helps you reset your expectations and will ultimately reduce your personal frustrations as you adjust.

Gap Analysis

The "gap" theory in quality management is this: whenever there is a mismatch between expectations and what actually happens, a gap is created. This gap is translated into customer disappointment, which then translates to bad word-of-mouth and lost repeat sales. If expectations are consistently exceeded, the reverse happens: customers are delighted, they come back for more, and they tell their friends.

The differences between your old and new positions may also expose some gaps. Whether you're moving from a large company to a small one, from the public sector to the private sector, or from a corporate position into consulting, the lay of the land will be different.

To help you, go through the following gap analysis. Using the chart below, list all the differences between your "old" and your "new" position, across each of the dimensions shown. Then for each of these differences, write down coping strategies and action items. Do this several days before you start, and then revise it several days after you have arrived. Awareness of the differences is the first step to dealing with them properly.

An example: if you have changed industries, a coping strategy might be to immerse yourself in knowledge about your new industry. Action items might be going to the library and getting several years' copies of the industry trade journals, soliciting your new colleagues' recommendations on the best books to read on the industry, and attending the annual trade conference. Financial analyst reports on the industry, company, and competitors can be helpful too.

Gap Analysis Chart

Dimension	Old Position	New Position	Coping Strategy	Action Items
Industry				
Organization size				
Organization structure				
Technology				
Processes – management				
Processes – accounting				
Processes – sales/marketing				
Processes – HR				
Processes – operations				
Job responsibilities				
Expectations of me				
External contact				
Workgroup size				
Resolving staff issues				
Relationships with staff				
Relationships with manager				

Expectations of Family and Friends

It is not just your own expectations that may need some readjustment. In your prior position, you may have left for the office early each morning and returned at a certain time each evening. By definition, you were *at* work, earning a living. If your new position demands travel, it is import to advise those around you as to what the "new normal" is. (It is also important to ensure that quality time with family and friends is not reduced, just moved around a bit.)

If your new position is one that has you working from a home office or with non-standard hours, you may find family and friends assuming that you are not working. Since you no longer go *to* work, they may assume that you no longer *do* work. You may find yourself deluged with requests to do home-based chores, pick up the kids, arrange for a service call, do the laundry, or any other number of non-work activities. Of course, you can choose to do as much of this as you wish. In fact, one of the reasons for your decision to leave the Mother Ship might indeed have been to spend more time with your family. This speaks once again to the importance of setting expectations properly: even though you might not be doing the same thing as before, you are most definitely working, and there are some boundaries that you can't cross.

A personal anecdote can illustrate this. We had just moved into a new house in a wonderful community. One of the features of the house was an oversized study on the main floor. My wife and I decided to share the study, so we could share computer peripherals and both have ready access to personal files. This worked out very well while I was still at the Mother Ship. When I left, it still worked out very well… during the day when no one was around. When my wife came home and decided to check her email in her half of the study, I found it completely impossible to concentrate on phone meetings or my own important work. For some reason, I always felt that she was looking over my shoulder, which of course, was not the case! How did we solve this problem? If the door to the study is closed, I am still at work, engaged in a phone meeting where I am not to be disturbed under any circumstance. Expectations set – expectations met.

A former colleague experienced this problem in a different way. She was in her mid-50s and had left the corporate world to become a free agent. She was busier than ever, consulting to a host of credible clients. Whenever she saw her friends, all of whom were still in the corporate world, she would be asked how retirement was going. This type of irritating comment, which implied that she was old and had little value left to give, took a while to eradicate.

Expectations also need to be set regarding your new compensation. Perhaps your new plan has bonuses distributed differently. Perhaps you are an entrepreneur, and you are in the "lean" start-up phase. Or perhaps you are a stock trader, building up your capital. Your family may see your business bank account with a large float and assume that this is for spending, rather than investment. If you are used to automatic deposits of a standard pay amount, getting used to a "lumpy" compensation plan may mean that you must also change *when* you spend your money.

Financial Success

If something isn't working exactly as you had originally planned, then change it, fast!

How much do you intend to make, and when? If you have a corporate position, are you on track to making your bonus? If you are an entrepreneur, how closely are you tracking to your budget? Letting those around you understand your objectives will help you to achieve them. If something isn't working exactly as you had originally planned, then change it, fast! Remember the importance of making mid-course corrections. Another wise idea: make sure that your business partners and spouse are up to speed as you make these changes. They have as much at stake in your success as you do.

Maintain and Rely on Your Network

Just because you are doing something new doesn't mean that your "old" network no longer has any value. While there are only so many hours during the day, time must be found to keep the network ticking. This doesn't mean the continuous knocking on doors looking for sales. And it doesn't mean a Christmas card each year. It means that each member of your network is on a specific contact cycle. Review Chapter 11 for the mechanics of doing this efficiently.

About the only time you might be excused for sending out a "broadcast" form letter to all your contacts is when you first land in your new position. It is the one time that you can brag, without appearing to be a braggart. Take the time to do it, hopefully within the first month of your arrival. On each letter, pen a short personal note to the recipient – they'll appreciate it. Maintaining your network is critical for your future as well. If you leave the Mother Ship once, you'll probably do it again.

Slowly Repair Your Damaged Bridges

Despite your best efforts, sometimes when you leave an organization, people are hurt, and they become upset with you. They may feel hard done by because of some tough decisions you made during your tenure. They may hold a grudge over a simple misunderstanding. Or they may have felt abandoned when you left. Because you are no longer there, you might not even be aware of the damaged bridges.

Grudges tend to fester and get worse with age.

Although time does heal wounds, grudges tend to fester and get worse with age. It takes very little effort to nurture damaged relationships back to health, and the time is well worth it. Particularly if you once worked well together, it may be that you can work together again sometime in the future. After all, it is a very small world. If you don't think you will ever work with that individual, in any type of relationship, be practical: a terribly negative relationship will spill poison on your reputation for years. Repair the bridge!

Focus

Every minute of the day has value, and unfortunately, each minute wasted is gone forever. For this reason more than anything else, each task you set yourself must be focused on driving your agenda forward. Busywork, procrastination, and half efforts are your worst enemies.

Most people, especially those successful in business, usually assume they have focus already. For the most part, they are right. But that doesn't mean improvement is impossible. Here are a few suggestions:

- Review your job objectives or your business plan a few weeks after you start. Ask yourself how many of your daily or weekly activities directly move you closer to achieving your goals.
- Write your objectives on a whiteboard or poster, mounted conspicuously in your office. Not only will the posting remind you of your goals, it will remind others as well.

- Which of your regular meetings are not productive, and why? Before they take even more of your time away, fix this problem.
- How much time is spent on political issues and what-might-be guessing, instead of driving to your goals? Politics and gossip can become a huge distraction, if left to run their course: stop them in their tracks.
- Which of your colleagues drain your time, either with mindless questions or because you have to fix their mistakes? In both cases, you have been taken away from your focus. Unfortunately, in both cases, your colleague doesn't have focus either.
- Review exactly how you spent your time the previous day. Where were the wasted minutes, and how can you avoid the wastage in the future?

Don't Lose Your Confidence: Remember Your Strengths

Disregard the naysayers and focus on your goals.

Even though much might have changed in your day-to-day life since you've left the Mother Ship, you are still the same person. It is very easy to lose confidence and begin to doubt your decision was the right one. It is okay to have these doubts. The first three months are especially challenging; give yourself time, and don't beat yourself up because of an occasional blip. It is easy for others to criticize from the sidelines, especially since they don't walk in your shoes each day. Disregard the naysayers and focus on your goals. Remember, there is no return without some degree of risk.

If you find it all a bit overwhelming, go back to those who have traditionally given you emotional and professional support, and ask for more. It is absolutely reasonable to tell them your concerns, and ask for their advice. Between those on your Reality Check Interview list, your mentors, your family, and your friends, there are plenty of folks who want to see you succeed. Giving them a chance to help you is useful for you, and sometimes very flattering for them.

After leaving a difficult organization, some people are so low that they have no confidence left to lose. One public-sector manager who left under these circumstances described the situation succinctly: "When I left, I *knew* that I could do nothing. When I got my first freelance contract, I couldn't believe it – I thought it was luck." If this is partly the case in your situation, look again at the exercise in self-labelling in Chapter 11. And remember that what underlies your past success will drive your future success too.

KEY POINTS

- Define yourself broadly by describing yourself along many dimensions.
- Dress for success.
- Reset your expectations, and while you're at it, reset those of your friends and family.
- Remember that your professional relationships can last a lifetime. Slowly repair your damaged bridges, and continue to build on the good relationships that you currently have.

ACTION CHECKLIST

❏ Gap Analysis

Chapter 14: Adjusting to the New Reality

Remember Your First Few Jobs

Remember your first full-time position? While you probably now recognize how green you were back then, see beyond that inexperience and recall what you did that helped you achieve your success. Although some people chalk it up to their luck, intelligence, or drive, most people will admit that their attitude had a lot to do with it.

What was *your* attitude back then? As a young person, you were allowed to be naive, asking dumb questions. You were expected to be keen. And it sure was appreciated when you rolled up your sleeves and attacked a problem with the rest of the team, without complaint. Fast-forward to today. Why can't you use these same attitudes in your new position?

ASK THE DUMB QUESTIONS: People will appreciate that you value their expertise.

BE KEEN: They will see your enthusiasm for the job, and it will be infectious.

ROLL UP YOUR SLEEVES: Your colleagues will see that you're one of the team – not an arrogant new hire from outside.

DON'T BE AFRAID OF MAKING MISTAKES: If you always play it safe, you'll never win the race. When an inevitable mistake occurs, take responsibility for it, learn from it, and then move on.

Isolation

In our old positions, we had a built-in, automated social network. People we didn't know so well greeted us warmly and exchanged pleasantries. Tight bonds of trust formed while working long hours on important projects. We developed real friendships with many people, socializing both after working hours, and while traveling on business.

In our new positions, even if we are moving into a corporate role, the workplace social-support network does not exist and must be developed, often from scratch. In an entrepreneurial position, your social network might not even include a single employee. If you are working from home, you must deal with both isolation and separation.

Isolation provides you an opportunity to focus, at precisely the time you need it most.

Isolation can be a real shock, but it can also be a real opportunity, as there is no hiding from it. You are forced to develop your workplace social network. The new people you meet will be both different and refreshing from what you're used to. Isolation also provides you an opportunity to focus, at precisely the time you need it most.

For those who feel the isolation most acutely (often entrepreneurs or caregivers) there are several practical things you can do to lessen any feelings of isolation you have:

- Schedule a minimum of three out-of-the-office meetings per week, with networking peers, suppliers, and prospects.
- If some of the work can be done at clients' or suppliers' premises, consider doing the work there, rather than at a home office.
- Remember that technology can also help. Whereas before you may have walked around the office to catch up with people, now you must do so electronically. Get used to using the telephone, email, and especially instant messaging to stay in contact with your clients, suppliers, and partners. Just remember, though, that electronic communication etiquette is a bit different than traditional communication etiquette. Nobody appreciates being interrupted by short emails that say "How's it going," no matter how friendly the intent.
- Review your after-hours activities, and slant them toward ones that give you the social interaction you are looking for. If you belong to a fitness club, for example, don't use the stationary bicycle by yourself – sign up for a group spinning class instead.

For those in new corporate positions, isolation is far easier to address. It can be as simple as sitting with different colleagues each day at lunch, to better understand their role in the organization.

Several years ago, my company appointed a new divisional president. As an outsider, he didn't really know anyone. One of his first objectives was to meet, either on the phone or in person, everyone in the organization. He set up visits to client sites, scheduled phone calls, meetings, breakfasts, lunches, and dinners. It took him about three months to do the rounds, but by then, he really understood the challenges and opportunities the company faced.

What did he talk about to those he met? He asked about their jobs, competitors, customers, challenges, and priorities.[11]

Where Did My Mentors Go?

The issue of your changed relationships with your mentors is coupled partly with the issue of isolation. As discussed earlier, after you leave, your internal mentors may feel that you are ungrateful. They may feel snubbed. Or they may feel that their role is to mentor people only for the good of the organization: with you gone, you no longer qualify for their time.

After you leave, your internal mentors may feel that you are ungrateful.

Nevertheless, if you feel there is benefit from the relationship, you should pursue an open, honest discussion with them on the subject. Recall how it was their mentoring over the years that developed your insight... which eventually led to your decision to leave. Let them know that you still value their insight and acumen and would like to maintain the relationship for mutual benefit. Listen to what they have to say. Finally, don't forget to include them in your schedule for follow-up.

11. Needless to say, these conversations should stick primarily to business. Many non-business topics will just cause you unnecessary trouble and shouldn't be discussed: politics, religion, and sexual orientation are examples.

However, you may wish to change whom you consider to be on your mentorship "A-List." You now find yourself in a new position – perhaps a new industry, role, company size, or location. If you could start from scratch, given your new reality, whom would you want as a mentor?

If you don't use your mentors, you lose them.

Starting a mentorship is straightforward, if you remember that it is a slow, mutual, step-by-step process. Ask your potential mentor for advice one day. Then ask them again some time later. Then ask them again some time after that. If the personal relationship develops at the same time as the professional one, you are on your way. Remember that not all people are cut out to be mentors, and not all who are capable are willing.

If you don't use your mentors, you lose them. Years ago, I developed a great relationship with my barber, Luigi. He was of the old school and always had some wisdom from his childhood that he was keen to pass on. For several years I hadn't seen him, as I had grown my hair and clearly didn't need a barber. When I returned to my usual monthly haircut, I asked for him at his shop and was greeted by the sad faces of his colleagues. Luigi had died six months earlier, of a stroke. He was in his early 60s. Sometimes you lose your mentors through no fault of your own, and when they are gone, their wisdom goes with them.

Reset Your Infrastructure

Your past success has been helped by the infrastructure around you. Sometimes this infrastructure is a technology department that quickly solves your problem, an assistant who handles your travel arrangements, or a graphic designer who makes your presentations beautiful. Other times the infrastructure is in the enterprise software that seemingly automates much of the bookkeeping.

In your new setting, these services may be delivered differently, or perhaps not at all. You might be expected to personally do things that were done by others in your previous position, or vice versa. Get used to asking questions that start with "Typically, how does one…" or "What is the fastest way to…".

If you are on your own or in a very small business, consider outsourcing as much of the infrastructure as possible to specialists in the field.

- Hire a bookkeeper instead of maintaining the accounting system yourself.
- Develop a good relationship with a full-service travel agency.
- Scout out a full-service print shop that can also do some basic graphic design.
- Ask some of your "independent" friends whom they use to help solve their computer problems. Asking the technical folks at your prior place of business for a referral might also make sense. There are plenty of clever, helpful technical folks out there: the problem is finding them.
- Professional recruiters, while they may be costly, may also be able to assist you with certain HR issues. If you are just looking for résumés, an on-line job board may be all you need.
- Insurance agents can help determine what additional coverage you may require and can often function as your entire pensions and benefits infrastructure.

Depending on your financing, you may not be able to afford any outside help. If this is the case, define the criteria for when you can afford it. For example, if an extra twelve hours a week can be reclaimed by hiring administrative help, and you use that time to increase sales, it makes sense to hire. If you can't afford to pay for a recruiter on day one, use the job boards until you can.

Role/Seniority

Differences can add up, whether it be in your title, role, industry, company size, or some other dimension. In your new position, don't make the assumption that you have the same power and authority as in your last one. After all, presumably much of your past authority was earned by you one step at a time. Your current authority, if you are in a corporate role, has been given to you along with your title, *but not yet earned*. Until you have earned the authority, expect a different dynamic when dealing with your colleagues, at least at the outset.

Differences beyond your personal position also have an impact, especially when dealing with external groups. If you used to be in a large company, your supplier contacts (and the services you received) were likely geared to the buying power of that larger company. While they would likely be polite to you if you contacted them for help, you might find yourself shunted to distributors who work only with smaller accounts such as yours. Of course, if you are moving to a larger business, or moving from one industry to another, your relationships are also likely to be changed. Review the Gap Analysis Chart in Chapter 13, and take a closer look at your Coping Strategies and Action Items. Are they still relevant, or do they need some finesse?

KEY POINTS

- Remember what it was like to start your first job. Rekindle that keen attitude!
- Whether you are moving to another Mother Ship, or are striking out on your own, you may experience feelings of isolation. This is to be expected, as both your workplace social network and your mentor relationships have been disrupted. Proactively address this by seeking social interaction within your new environment, and outside of it. Take advantage of the pause, and consider whom you really want (and need) to have as your mentors.
- Change has also occurred elsewhere. You have a new role and you work within a different infrastructure. Keep your mind open to different ways of doing things, and take advantage of the unique advantages of your situation.

Chapter 15: Special Ideas for Entrepreneurs

Board of Advisers

If you now hold the most senior position in an organization, expect a certain isolation in the role. Your staff may not want to "bother" you with all the issues of the day. And many of your issues cannot be openly discussed with them. Yet to be successful, you need their input, and you need strategic counsel as well. Where to get it?

One of the primary goals of the Advisory Board is to widen the experience of the leader.

All incorporated entities are required to have a Board of Directors. Small and medium-sized private companies often do have a "Board," but it often doesn't do much more than approve financial statements, if even that. The Advisory Board concept takes on some of the functions of a public company board of directors, tailored to the special requirements of the entrepreneurial executive.

One of the primary goals of the Advisory Board is to widen the experience of the leader and, by extension, to bring greater depth to the management team. In smaller companies, this may provide the leader with a coterie of experts-on-call. In larger enterprises, the Advisory Board can also provide questions for the leader to ask of his or her team. Here are some of the other functions that the Advisory Board can play:

- Help with strategic planning.
- Provide management perspective during times of change.
- Act as management coach.
- Force additional accountability on the CEO.
- Provide management with experience working with a more sophisticated structure.
- By virtue of the names on the board, provide some marketplace credibility.

Building Your Team

How do you decide that the time is right to hire your next staff member? There are two competing approaches that you might consider:

- Hire for prospective growth, and then sell like crazy to use your new capacity;
- Sell like crazy, until everyone is working overtime, and then hire to relieve the pressure.

Which approach you follow depends on a number of factors, including the cost of overtime, the availability of staff to work overtime, and how long it takes to get your staff up to speed. Of course, your self-confidence and your financing have a lot to do with it as well.

No matter when you hire, you have to consider very carefully the skills of the person you hope to hire.

- Is it an administrator, to deal with the mundane and allow you to focus on what you do best?
- Is it someone with a different skill base (e.g., you are marketing – they are finance) to allow you to cope with growth more effectively?
- Is it someone exactly like yourself, since your "recipe" has worked very effectively?
- Is it someone who has worked in a small company, to complement your big-company experience (or vice versa)?

Each situation is unique, but you might consider the following exercise useful: lay out the organization chart for 5, 10, and 25 employees. Then, for each position on each chart, assign a number that indicates the order of hiring.

Keep Costs Variable

Perhaps, having lived on a *large* Mother Ship for so long, you haven't considered all the different ways that a task can get done. You are probably more comfortable hiring employees. But there are other ways to skin the cat. Hire a short-term consultant or a longer-term contractor. Outsource. Use a temp agency. Set up a joint venture with a partner company. And on it goes.

Especially at the outset, when your sustained need for staff is uncertain, it is critical to match your expenses with your revenues. This means that you must keep your costs variable. Even if the cost over the shorter run is more expensive, it reduces your risk immeasurably.

Own what is strategic, outsource everything else.

On the other hand, you should absolutely hire employees, instead of outsourcing or hiring variable capacity, when the task is strategic to your business. Own what is strategic (processes, patents, relationships), outsource everything else.

Hiring employees will allow knowledge to grow within your business; this knowledge can then develop value in and of itself. For example, customer service personnel with knowledge of many past versions of a product can often solve problems faster than an outsourced call center relying on a database. Sales staff with strong customer relationships can relay important market intelligence back to you; independent sales agents cannot. In fact, independent sales agents often will own the customer relationship so completely that you may not even know the end customers' names!

Change and the Trap of Arrogance

Most managers recognize that as a business grows, there must be changes to the people, processes, and systems. After all, the needs of a smaller regional distributor are very different than the national distributor the company grew up into.

After years of success, how do you know *you* are the right person to lead the organization to the next level? Maybe you are, maybe you're not. Don't fall into the arrogance trap of assuming that you will always be the right one to lead your new enterprise. Your Advisory Board can help you answer this question, if it is asked to do so.

What is the arrogance trap? One arrogance trap is the fear of delegating to your staff, just in case they make a Terrible Mistake. Another is the mistaken belief that you yourself are the reason for your new business's success, and therefore you don't need to listen to, nor solicit, others' advice.

Consider: as soon as you stop listening to your customers, employees, partners, and suppliers, you will never learn what it takes to address their needs. You'll have only your assumptions and guesses to rely on. If you spend all your time talking, there is no time for listening! Only by listening will you be able to make the many mid-course corrections that are required to steer a new enterprise to successful waters.

KEY POINTS

- If you're by yourself, it doesn't mean you have to do everything yourself. While you might not have the infrastructure of the large organization, surround yourself with the expertise that you need, but do your best to keep your costs variable.
- Consider setting up a formal advisory board: it can help you maintain focus and provide important feedback on strategic issues.
- Listen to your customers, suppliers, and employees.

Chapter 16: Long-Term Tomorrow

Most successful people are driven. If the goal of the change you have just made (or are considering making) is to "get rich quick" and then retire, you're missing the point. The journey should be just as exciting, if not more so, than the destination. Excepting lottery winners, most people who "get rich quick" enjoy what they're doing and usually get rich as a by-product of the passion they have for what they do. To those who strive only for the goal and not the journey – you're missing half the fun.

The Role of Sabbaticals

What is a sabbatical? It can be either a short break (two to three months) or one that is longer, often up to a year. It is a time that can be used to disconnect from your normal work patterns and reconnect to your priorities. Some companies have sabbatical programs, but a sabbatical is often taken between jobs, or perhaps as an unpaid leave from a long-term employer. Needless to say, the more senior you are, the tougher it is for the employer to fill your shoes while you are away, and therefore the less likely that they would allow you to leave for an extended period.

Many people spend hours considering their retirement plans. They dream of golfing all day. Then sitting on a charitable board in the evening. Spending months each year traveling. At the same time, they'll learn to play the piano, write a book, and spend more time with their spouse.

There is a good chance, however, that you will be disappointed with some of the realities of retirement. What if you can't do it all? Arthritis plagues your fingers, so learning the piano is out. Fatigue may limit your evening activities. And unfortunately, your spouse has long developed his or her own interests, separate from yours, because of all the time you spent at work. Or even worse, you (or your spouse) may succumb to ill health and not even make it to retirement.

Taking a sabbatical gives you the opportunity to do some of these "fun" things now, while you still have the inclination, energy, and health.

WHERE IS THE VALUE OF A BREAK? Consider: you can spend up to 40 years of your life working, and then have 20 years of retirement. Would three months (or one year) not be more valuable earlier in life than at retirement? Yes! So why don't more people take sabbaticals? The answer: people don't take sabbaticals for the same reason they don't leave the Mother Ship. It is tough to find the courage, and there are plenty of "reasons" to stay.

Hopefully, by this point in the book, you will have developed enough courage to understand that there is life beyond the Mother Ship, and that the same drive that gave you your success on the ship will power you after you leave it.

Three-Month Sabbatical

Recharge, achieve short-term goals, reconnect with family and friends, and evaluate possible alternative career paths.

What should you do when you take three months of your retirement and spend it earlier on a sabbatical? Certain things come to mind: recharge, achieve short-term goals, reconnect with family and friends, and evaluate possible alternative career paths.

At the beginning of the sabbatical, you may feel disconnected from the hectic nature of your previous position. Your workplace social network will no longer exist. You will not have the deadlines and the demands of a day-to-day position. And you may find time starting to slip by faster than you think.

For all these reasons, it is critically important to set clear objectives for yourself, and set a firm weekly schedule. Here's a suggestion for setting your objectives: start with your Personal Balance Sheet (Chapter 8), and see what comes to mind. If you are closer to retirement age, also consider if there is a certain activity or routine that you would like to test-drive prior to actually retiring.

In addition to any ideas generated by your Personal Balance Sheet, it will be important to set two additional objectives for yourself:

1. Satisfy your need for a social network. This might be as simple as going out for several networking lunches each week or getting involved in your children's schools.
2. Decide, by the end of the sabbatical, what your next step will be. Re-read this book, and re-do the exercises within it. You will find that time off has given you a more focused perspective on your personal and professional goals.

Setting objectives for your sabbatical can help you answer questions from your curious (and likely jealous) friends and former colleagues. More importantly, it will give you a sense of purpose. At the end of your sabbatical, you will be able to look back and point to specific, achieved accomplishments.

One-Year Sabbatical

With a year break, you can try something very different, often with your family: travel abroad, study, etc. You can possibly complete a major life goal, such as completing an advanced degree or undertaking a physical challenge. You can also test out a potential retirement routine and tweak it to something that is appealing.

Set objectives and a schedule for yourself.

Because of the significant length of time that you are away from the workforce, it is even more important to set objectives and a schedule for yourself. Even if it seems too "business-like," spend a few minutes each month ensuring that you are on track to achieving your objectives. If you aren't, either change your activities or change your objectives.

Entrepreneurial friends of mine, after selling their company, decided that a one-year sabbatical would give them a fresh life experience. After considering several alternatives, they moved to Beijing. They now attend university there as full-time students, learning Mandarin during the week and sightseeing each weekend. The whole world was their oyster, and they chose China!

Whether your sabbatical is three months long or twelve, at some point you will return to the workforce. While your new post-sabbatical role will be exciting, you may also feel a sense of loss. Consider the objectives and activities you set for yourself while you were away. Maybe you had set goals relating to personal fitness and spending time with your family. Will the end of your sabbatical also mean spending less time with your family and gaining back all that weight? Hopefully not, but there are only so many hours in the day, and something has to give.

Your Personal Balance Sheet can help set your priorities post-sabbatical.

Before you return to the working world, get out your Personal Balance Sheet and update it. Although you might not have time to do everything on your return, defining your priorities will help you achieve at least a modicum of balance. And help keep that extra weight off.

Maternity or Parental Leave

Each jurisdiction has different laws regarding maternity or parental leave; your employer likely has policies that will affect you as well. If you will be taking time off to care for a new child, your priorities will be highly focused on your new responsibilities. But are there other personal or professional objectives you want to consider at the same time? Especially if you see this leave as a transition into the next step of your career, actively using your break is critical.

"I Can't Do It Because I Can't Afford It"

It is always easier to close doors than to think how to walk through them. From a financial standpoint, it seems that the "hit" taken from losing three months' salary is substantial. You might be thinking to yourself that it is tough to make ends meet as it is. But really, in 480 months of a typical career, can you not find three months to take a break?

From a purely practical standpoint, financing a sabbatical requires some planning and forethought. Here are some ideas to consider:

- **REALISTICALLY ESTIMATE LOWER EXPENDITURE LEVELS.** Plan to put yourself on a strict budget while away from the workforce, but test it out beforehand to see if you can live with it. Consider what you might be able to give up or replace with cheaper alternatives (expensive restaurant meals, for example).
- **IF YOU HAVE A MORTGAGE, NEGOTIATE TO REDUCE YOUR PAYMENTS.** This can be done by extending the amortization, reducing the rate, or both. Often, this is the biggest single expenditure that one has, and reducing payments for a few months can provide the highest relief. Make sure, though, that you can increase payments back to a higher amount once the sabbatical is over.
- **SAVE YOUR VACATIONS.** In the period before your sabbatical, don't use any of your vacation – save it to help fund your time off. If you currently have four weeks' annual leave and you are able to get by without any vacation throughout this year at all, then *one-third of your three-month sabbatical is already paid for.* If you have a longer amount of accrued vacation, it looks even better.
- **REVIEW YOUR INSURANCE PLANS.** Are there savings that can be generated by reviewing your life and disability insurance? Are there cheaper plans that offer the same types of coverage? (And while you are away on sabbatical, what is the cost of medical, dental, and other health coverage?)

  It is useful to point out that there are often other hidden savings that we can access. Some insurance policies, for example, have a cash value that grows each month. Can your policy be collapsed and replaced with a policy that provides coverage but doesn't include a savings component? (Or failing that, can you "borrow" your own money from the plan, at a preferential interest rate?)
- **RAID YOUR SAVINGS.** Although this doesn't sound exactly appealing to most people, it is truly a matter of perspective. If you consider your sabbatical as part of your retirement, but taken earlier, where is the harm in spending some of your

retirement savings earlier as well? Of course, the financially minded will point out that any money taken from retirement savings is money that cannot grow over time. And of course, they'd be right. If you decide to raid your retirement savings, you should consider all the consequences and govern yourself accordingly. If you have a rainy day fund, a sabbatical would certainly qualify as a worthwhile place to use it.

Consider a Permanent Move

An international assignment can give greater depth to your knowledge.

The decision to pull up all your roots and move to another part of the world is both a scary and an exciting prospect. Although a full discussion of this type of move is beyond the scope of this book, many of the analytical tools (Personal Balance Sheet, for example) can set the context as to whether a permanent move makes sense.

Purely from a career standpoint, taking an international assignment can give greater depth to your knowledge, and may be a necessary step for your advancement.

Another reason to consider a permanent move is for retirement planning purposes. If you hope to eventually retire to another city, you may judge it worthwhile to move there beforehand in order to make local friendships and social connections.

If you are looking to move first, then hope to find your next position when you are on the ground, don't deceive yourself. It is not easy. Consider that the cultural norms and business practices may be very different from what you're used to at home. Your personal network is more geographically bound to where you are now. Even your professional credentials may not be recognized in the new location. For peace of mind, budget for a longer job search.

If you are considering moving to another city to be closer to family or if you are considering a position that is located elsewhere, the question of *where* has been decided for you. If you're not sure where you'd like to relocate to, the argument for taking a sabbatical, purely to test a potential landing spot, is even more appealing.

Priorities and Life Goals

If I were to die tomorrow, what is the one thing I'd be sorry I hadn't done? And if I were to die next week, next month, or next year?

Each of these questions helps quickly prioritize what we might want to do next. For tomorrow, the answer might be to tell your spouse or children that you loved them. Next week? Maybe you always wanted to see a part of the world, and there's just enough time to do it. If you knew you were to die next month, maybe you would want to use the time to develop better relationships with your friends and family. Maybe work on a personal legacy project.

How many of these possibilities involve your work or career?

What to do if you were to die next year is a little tougher, but only because the possibilities widen greatly. But consider: how many of these possibilities involve your work or career? Likely very few. This is why thinking about the long-term tomorrow is so connected with how we use each and every day. With so much of our day filled with our jobs, shouldn't our careers complement, not clash with, our life goals? "Today" is your opportunity to start doing what matters.

When I'm on my deathbed and look back, will I be satisfied with what I've accomplished?

Another ugly question: on your deathbed, will you really value those late nights at the office, or will the pain of remembering missed children's birthday parties be on your mind? Will you be satisfied with what you've accomplished, or will you wonder how you wasted so much time on unimportant matters? Will you be satisfied with a tombstone that says "Always met his deadlines"?

Consider once again your Personal Balance Sheet. At the end of your life, would you not want it to read "Mission Accomplished"? If so, then the only thing that separates you from achievement is time, and how you use it.

Career Maturity

Our career really started in school. While learning the technical subjects, we also discovered what we enjoyed and what we were good at. For many of us, the subjects we took were forced upon us, with little choice. That was appropriate, as we didn't yet have the maturity, nor the life experience, to advocate for greater choice. The higher up the educational ladder we went, the more choice and specialization was available to us.

When we got our first job, we continued learning, and as we mastered each skill, we were rewarded with one promotion after another. Some of these jobs were enjoyable, while others we viewed only as stepping stones for something even better.

At a certain point, though, the opportunities and the rewards within our organization begin to have less appeal. The first part of *Leaving the Mother Ship* provides many reasons for this, but one reason stands out. With more experience, we have developed the maturity to know what we want: in life and in our career.

You may have felt this way, but were uneasy expressing it, let alone doing something about it. The SkillChecks, Job Quality Check, Personal Balance Sheet, and other tools helped to crystallize your thoughts and present them in a way that translates knowledge into action.

You feel empowered. You are no longer willing to delegate control over your career to others. If you leave the Mother Ship once, you have proven you have the strength of mind to achieve any goal you set for yourself.

KEY POINTS

- Sabbaticals can be useful time-outs to recharge your energy, test new directions, or reconnect with family or friends. If you decide to take one, make sure that you set clear objectives for yourself. Objectives provide structure to your time away, and when achieved, leave you with confidence and pride.
- Your career should help you achieve your life goals. Don't spend so much time on your job that there is no time for much of anything else. Use every minute of every day productively, for once time passes, it can't be recaptured.
- By going through the exercises in this book every two years (or whenever there is a major change in your life) you have the tools to master your destiny, both on the job and in your life.

Afterword

Everyone will change their job at some point, even if it is at the point of retirement.

The only question is *who* decides *when* that change will take place. While your managers, mentors, family, and friends can all provide advice, when it comes to leaving the Mother Ship, it is you who must stand up and say, "This is what I want." If it is not you who decides what is next (and best) for you, it *will* be someone else – and the question of *when* will be answered by their schedule, not yours.

Life is not a dress rehearsal.
Don't just *Leave the Mother Ship,* be the captain of it!

Keynotes, Workshops, Resources

Interested in *Leaving the Mother Ship* resources? Sign up for Leaving the Mother Ship news and information at www.LeavingTheMotherShip.com, and gain access to templates and resources to help you on your journey.

Looking for a keynote or seminar that will move your audience to action? Contact seminars@LeavingTheMotherShip.com for information on Randall Craig's latest seminars and keynotes:

For Employers:

- Retaining and promoting your best: making the Mother Ship fast, fun, and profitable.
- Change the odds by changing the rules!
- Up or out: marketing and business development for professional service firms.

For Employees:

- Achieve! Life! Balance!
- Why not? Thinking outside the career box.
- From Knowledge to Action: starting a successful business.
- Give yourself permission: How to carve time for yourself.
- Leaving the Mother Ship: Having the courage to leave, and charting the path to get there.

Interested in the one day *Leave the Mother Ship!* workshop in your area? Attending this dynamic workshop will empower you to take the next step in your career. In addition to the material covered in the book, get feedback on how the process should be customized for you. Learn how to break down the barriers that prevent you from achieving your goals. Enrich your experience with others who have successfully left the Mother Ship. Leave the workshop with more focus, direction and the drive to get things done. For more information, contact workshop@LeavingTheMotherShip.com.

Looking for bulk copies of Leaving the Mother Ship?
Special rates are available for bulk purchases.
Contact our publisher with quantities and date needed, at specialsales@KnowledgeToActionPress.com.

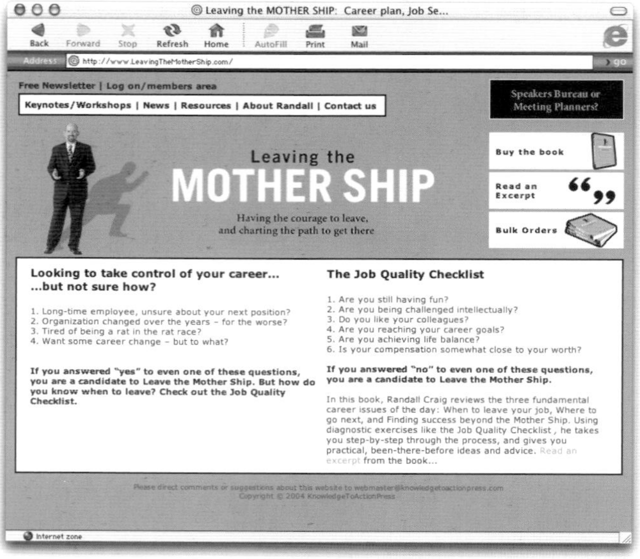

www.LeavingTheMotherShip.com